ACHEBE AND THE POLITICS
OF REPRESENTATION

ACHEBE AND THE POLITICS OF REPRESENTATION

FORM AGAINST ITSELF,

FROM COLONIAL CONQUEST

AND OCCUPATION TO POST-INDEPENDENCE

DISILLUSIONMENT

ODE OGEDE

Africa World Press, Inc.

P.O. Box 1892
Trenton, NJ 08607

P.O. Box 48
Asmara, ERITREA

Africa World Press, Inc.

P.O. Box 1892
Trenton, NJ 08607

P.O. Box 48
Asmara, ERITREA

Cover design: Jonathan Gullery
Book design: Wanjiku Ngugi

Library of Congress Cataloging-in-Publication Data

Ogede, Ode.
    Achebe and the politics of representation / by Ode Ogede
      p. cm.
    Includes bibliographical references (p.) and index.
    ISBN 0-86543-774-2--ISBN 0-86543-775-0 (pbk.)
      1. Achebe, Chinua--Political and social views. 2. Politics and literature--Nigeria--History--20th century. 3. Representative government and representation in literature. 4. Representative government and representation --Nigeria. 5. Political fiction--History and criticism. 6. Nigeria--In literature. I. Title

PR9387.9.A3 Z847 2000
823--dc21

99-088673

CONTENTS

ACKNOWLEDGMENTS

I wish to express my appreciation to the friend, who, when first reading an early draft of the essay that later became this book, offered comments that positively guided me throughout the work's preparation. Because Achebe is held in unusual affection and respect by his readers, he cautioned me, I would need to write more persuasively than is customary about the issues I wanted to raise. In a revisionary text that challenges firmly held opinions about a prodigious and towering literary figure, the need to write cogently should be obvious enough. But the need for good writing and factual accuracy is a warning that has made me aware that I may be seen as a fool who has dared to dance on spaces where angels fear to thread even lightly. I do not conceive of my role as an adversarial one. However, since objectivity is such a hotly contested issue in the humanities today, it is clear that some readers will cast me in that role despite my intention to offer what must be the first comprehensive critical study of Achebe's view of colonization and its aftereffects.

Although all views expressed here, of course, are my own and should not be attributed in any way to the people who have assisted me, I want enthusiastically to thank my most influential teachers at Ahmadu Bello University: John Agi, Brian Downse, Donald J. Cosentino, Michael Etherton, Ahmed Issouf, Brian T. Last, Mbulelo Mzamane, Robert Ness, Kuhara Ndahi, Festus O. Ogunlade, Virginia Ola, Grace Shortland, and Michael Ward. I have been inspired by their teaching beyond even their own imagining. I am also grateful to the Andrew W. Mellon Foundation and the University of Pennsylvania, which funded this project along with my other ongoing work on the African novel. For his support at a critical moment in my career, I owe a huge debt to Eugene A. Eaves, Provost and Vice-Chancellor for Academic Affairs at North Carolina Central University. I want to thank Chris Lorrey and Patricia Allen, for improving my prose. My gratitude also goes to F. Odun Balogun, F. Abiola Irele, Isidore Okpewho, and Rosemarie Mitsch, who continue to inspire me with their dedication and commitment to scholarship. Colleagues past and present, including Otegwu Ewule, Philemon Gomwalk, Ebow Mensah, Charles Nnolim, and Ode Ojowu of Ahmadu Bello University, Herman Beavers and Al Filreis of University of Pennsylvania, Marilyn Button and Ropo Sekoni of Lincoln University, Julene Fuller, Mary Mathew, Muriel Mellown, Arthrell Sanders, and Ruth Kennedy of North Carolina Central University also provided intellectual and emotional stimulation. The late John Sekora contributed to this work by welcoming me with open arms to Durham and by offering warm support throughout our time together. Jonathan Haynes of Long Island University read a number of chapters, and though clearly disagreeing with my opinions, he offered advice that helped to strengthen and sustain this book. For their further assistance, I also wish to thank my friends and family: Egbe Adulugba, Jairus Edeh, Egboja Agi, Agi Ajochi, Bryan Curtain, Mrs. Lydia Ediah, Ochi Ikape, Micah Idah, Rev. Ogbale Ikoni, Edugbeke Ode, Ona Ode, Okeh Odeh, Edugbeke Ogede, Mrs. Comfort Ogiri, Okwute Oibe, Ode Okoh, Idu Onah, and Ian Strachan. Librarians at Van Pelt Library at the University of Pennsylvania, Davis at the University of North Carolina at Chapel Hill, and Shepard at North Carolina Central University were a great help. Most of all, I wish to thank my wife Shianyisimi and our children Ochuole, Ogede Jr., and Michael, who kept me good company during my stay in Philadelphia, when the first draft of the manuscript was completed in the summer of 1995. This book is dedicated to them and to my cousin John Okwe Ajochi, who saw to it that I received a formal education despite many obstacles.

INTRODUCTION

The study that follows is an examination of colonialism and its aftermath—i.e., the self-rule that followed resistance efforts in Africa—as reconfigured in the fiction of Nigerian writer Chinua Achebe. Not only is he Africa's best-known novelist, Achebe is among those prominent imaginative writers from formerly colonized territories interested in uncovering and documenting the way that brought his society under the domination of foreign rule. This event has traumatized Africa as no other, and the continent has yet to recover completely. Bearing in mind that Achebe has said he intended his work to fill gaps in historical reconstruction, one question immediately came to mind as I began to read his works: Is there any way that a creative writer such as Achebe, from a formerly colonized territory, could have used the colonizers's tongue and idioms without reproducing some of their stereotypes of the indigenous people?

Whether utilizing indigenous or imported forms as part of the mission to reverse the specious identity inscribed by the former master, literature has traditionally been viewed as a purely moral activity that requires no justification. A careful reading of some of the works of these exploratory writers, however, suggests that much of their labor has been from the beginning contradictory and self-defeating, evincing some of the difficulty involved in separating method from its related assumptions. Achebe's works, long considered as good examples of expert storytelling, can also be seen as limited by the unsuitability of their informing vision. One understands that satire and tragedy, his principle tools of imaginative expression, are not merely innocent aesthetic frameworks; rather, they are superstructures that express core Western ideas and attitudes.

That Western notions color the vision of some of Achebe's works demonstrates that, although resistance writing might be an enormously important affair, the spirit and sophistication of the writer is

as critical as the philosophy and tools he brings to the entire enterprise. The present study evaluates the viability of accepting such
works as innocent stories or as mere exercises in formalism, as
indeed the author himself asks us to do. One must examine them
for traces of a maudlin act, where a mixture of incompatible elements lay hidden. Satire and tragedy were originally employed by
the European conquerors for dehumanizing the African subject;
hence when Achebe attempted to extrapolate the forms from their
original contexts, using them in his quest for identity reconstruction,
they were bound, willy-nilly, to be ineffective devices for liberation.
This is not surprising, since satire and tragedy have never had an
unfettering role. Once Achebe chose to implement these imperialist forms, he placed himself directly in the trap set by the conqueror,
making it possible for him to perpetuate some of the very imperialist clichés that he was trying to combat. As to what the specific
nature of his influences are, we may never know. However, in a
careful reading of his works readers can discern where Achebe
decided to play the role of a simple native informant and then either
resolved to recount historical and cultural events accurately or to
repress and disfigure them.[1]

Over the years many fine books have been written on the subject of social vision, gender, and politics in black Africa. Cultural
clashes—e.g., tradition versus modernity, urban versus rural, individualism versus communalism, as well as the fusion of cultures,
and cultural nationalism, traditional African values, social change,
the problems of self-rule (commonly known as the post-independence disillusionment), are themes often recycled. However, the
image of the colonial encounter constructed by African writers has
suffered relative critical neglect.[2] Nevertheless, the modern nations of black Africa all have their existence inextricably bound up
with colonialism, not only in their origin but in their structures of
tutelage that were devised under colonial rule. Since colonization is
responsible for most, if not for all, of the experiences that have
altered the basis of black African societies—as well as the humanity of African peoples—it is also responsible for laying the very
foundation of their modern literatures. It is important to understand
how this process evolved, how it has affected black Africans, and
how they have attempted to contain it in order to develop a deeper

knowledge of contemporary Africa and its literature.

This literary study explicating the representation of colonization in black African fiction uniquely looks to the past not with a desire to re-write it, but to understand better the experiences that created the present-day African.[3] Social scientists provide insight into many aspects of colonization and the post-independence experiences of Africans. However, these sources often ignore the lives of everyday people and their emotions. They overlook much that is critical to human existence: love, anger, fear, frustration, fulfilment, hope, a sense of achievement or defeat are better conveyed in fiction. There one can see that what happens to the individual is every bit as influential as confrontations between groups or nations over territory.

I see historical accuracy or authenticity as a legitimate principle for evaluating literary works which claim to be historically-based. Works showing an immoderate departure, as some of Achebe's ocassionally do, from the range of what is conventionally verifiable, i.e., facts and trends documented elsewhere by objective recorders, cannot legitimately lay claim to historical authenticity. Furthermore, creative works that are inordinately obsessed with oratory at the expense of fact yield too readily to the seductive pull of fantasy. To be so enamored with the act of storytelling itself trivializes the reality of human misery, demonstrating profound insensitivity.

Insofar as the role of native informant is always a suspect one, it is within the province of a committed theory of literature to show how someone writing during an era dominated by colonialist literature could avoid providing markedly derivative colonialist fiction. For a writer to approach such a subject as the terror wrought by colonization with humor or ease or casualness is to be wanting in a lack of feeling for human dignity. Since the publication of *Things Fall Apart*, African literature, including Achebe's art, has advanced, both in the variety of its themes and of its modes of expression. Many Western readers are captivated by *Things Fall Apart*, because for them it stands firmly as a delightful relic of the familiar tradition of Aristotelian or Greek tragedy. That tragedy contains formulaic patterns, i.e., diminishing the capacity of Achebe's works for realistic representation, is too often ignored. Ironically, the aesthetic qualities responsible for the staying power of *Things Fall*

Apart have undermined its claims to being committed literature. Nevertheless, if I can expand readers' interest in Achebe beyond that first novel, I will have met my primary objective in this study. Indeed my purpose is not only to call attention to the irony of Achebe's having relied on modes that limit the power of his earliest fiction to instruct and to promote resistance but also to inspire readers to consider the accomplishment Achebe has made in later texts, which have remained largely overlooked though they demonstrate the extraordinary range of his creative intelligence.

Chapter 1

THE LIMITS OF OPPOSITIONALITY WITHIN LANGUAGE AND FORMS IMPOSED BY COLONIZATION

(DILEMMAS FACED BY ERSTWHILE COLONIZED PERSONS ATTEMPTING TO WRITE IN THE IDIOMS OF THE FORMER MASTERS)

Here is the primary question: Can a writer from a once colonized region address his former masters through their own idioms without being complicit in their politics of narration? It is a question that invites another that is equally critical, although continually unexpressed: Why are there so few analyses of African writers' fictionalized accounts of the colonial conquest that compare them with the accounts of social scientists? [1] Even if we cannot make the outright claim that modern African literature was created by colonialism, we can say without hesitation that the circumstances that arose as a result of colonization provoked this literature's primary subject matter. Though literary critics have neglected to explore the topic exhaustively, colonization is not peripheral to modern life or literature in Africa. The consequencies of colonization are still in evidence, and this permeates most of black Africa's literary efforts. Exploring the way a major figure such as Chinua Achebe has constructed his fiction, i.e., portraying both the occurrence and the aftermath of colonization, should offer an exceptionally heightened means of understanding the one enterprise that affected (and continues to affect) real human beings, whose lives it has changed (and continues to change), in unique and momentous ways.

Achebe is unmistakably one of the African writers who have added most significantly to the Africanist discourse on the imperial project.[2] Justly celebrated as a central figure in modern African literature, he was one of the first African writers to compose detailed fictional narratives about the experience of colonization. David Carroll, one of the most dependable critics of his works, links Achebe's leadership in African literature to the fact that Achebe was the first African writer to seriously use a modern literary form—the novel—to confront the questions of identity and representation that arose out of the colonial encounter. Carroll's position is supported by many other critics, including Oladele Taiwo, Simon Gikandi, Odun Balogun, G. D. Killam, Kofi Owusu, and Emmanuel Ngara.[3]

Historians such as Obaro Ikime, Ade Ajayi, Omer Cooper, Adu Boahen, and Elizabeth Isichei have led us to an understanding of colonization as a swirling movement that affected the indigenous aristocracy; but what of what happened to ordinary citizens as they struggled to order their lives from day to day under those chaotic circumstances? What happened to ordinary people in such unsettled and unsettling situations? How did they find food, find spouses, raise a family and children, organize their lives on a daily basis? How did they preserve their sanity in circumstances of such utter turmoil? Conventional historians have been woefully silent on this subject. It is refreshing to turn to fiction and find abundant information about the experiences of average people.

Achebe has had little to say about Arab colonization throughout the Sahara and southwards (but then neither have the conventional historians). He has, however, particularly marshalled an astonishing array of details concerning the confrontation between Africans, the Igbos specifically, and Europeans from across the Atlantic.[4] What follows is an examination of how his fictional recollections tally in essential details with parallel records about many of the same events kept by historians, anthropologists, and political scientists.

Achebe takes the moral questions for granted, describing his task as residing merely in indigenization of a foreign language like English. The dispute, however, definitely goes well beyond this, touching as it does on questions about the accuracy of his facts and the worldview projected in his work. While an author may score high marks for his effort to "indigenize" a foreign language, the ideological dimension of that message is still a question; the writer's intentional claims cannot be accepted uncritically. In his first novel (*Things Fall Apart*), Achebe adopts an uncompromising stance in his criticism of the failings of the indigenous African leadership, while the atrocities of colonization are all too clearly relegated to a secondary focus. Why does he do this? Why does he make excuses for the weaknesses of the colonizers, while spewing undiluted venom at Africans for failing to rule with conscience? Why does he fail to hold the colonizing powers to the same standard of morality, especially since colonialism is initially responsible for creating the majority of the problems with which the indigenous leadership has found itself beset? Could it be that the attempt to exonerate the brutality of the occupation forces issues from a stance Achebe has contrived with deliberation? If so, is he one of those writers who uphold the belief that the moral properties of human beings are genetically determined? Does Achebe present colonialism with such a demonstratively forgiving spirit because he believes its proponents are inherently less capable of moral sentience than the conquered people?

Joseph Conrad used a similar technique to justify the moral failings of the European protagonists in his African fiction. If Achebe's writing has similar characteristics, to what degree are the artistic modes of expression responsible?[5] Let us remember the roles British colonial authors bestowed on satire and tragedy in promoting policies of subjugation. Since the tragic mode is inherently a manner of acceptance of imperfection, an acquiescent mode that accepts the status quo (while satire unflinchingly is a mode of rejection of foibles), it should have been clear from the beginning that African writers should employ satire and tragedy with an extreme sense of discretion. That Achebe employs tragedy to depict the activities of the colonizing forces and the immediate African response while utilizing satire to blast the post-independence African leadership shows the misdirection of his early work; he holds himself hostage within colonialist discourses of fiction. An inversion of the direction of their uses would be more appropriate.

The novelistic practice adopted in works like *Things Fall Apart* and *No Longer at Ease*, which take the conventional tragic form, and in *A Man of the People*, which depends on the customary satiric line, raises the question of whether an African writer who works uncritically within Western forms can escape some of the alienating attitudes that accompany them. Other works, such as *Arrow of God*, *Anthills of the Savannah*, and *Girls at War and Other Stories*—which hold their informing satiric and tragic elements in better balance—achieve results that are far less wrongheaded. This demonstrates how tragedy and satire are problematic not only as imported modes but as ones that package experience, effectively reduce roles, and cast people into predetermined slots. These are snares for which the African writer would be wise to be vigilant.

It is not only naive but misleading to attach a tragic quality to a situation like colonization. To do so is to give an approving nod to the whole messy affair and to invest it with a false sense of predestination. We do not know why Achebe did not explore an alternative strategy. Recognizing the pivotal role that the issue of representation's purpose has commanded in modern criticism, the critic W. J. T. Mitchell reminds us that "even purely 'aesthetic' representation of fictional persons or events can never be completely divorced from political and ideological questions." [6] Since Achebe's principal goal is to use literary forms in a bid to capture that momentuous historic epoch when the contact of two cultures changed the lives of his people, the connection between his aesthetics and his politics is critical.

Achebe has consistently identified himself as a strategist of decolonization, as one who utilizes literature to further cultural resistance to colonialism. However, the true test of theory is in practice. Achebe has claimed cultural assertion to be the main motivation for his writing, yet he continues to face a problem that confronts every writer from the formerly colonized territory; the problem of how to achieve a novelty of representation and inscribe what is truly revolutionary within forms that were originally meant for retrogressive missions. This is not an easy task to carry out.

As demonstrated in his early work, Achebe has failed at these tasks. He was not radical enough as an inventor—he borrowed too much from Western liberalism. And his political consciousness was merely oppositional. The lack of impact on the scale desired is thus not surprising, for, as Ross Chambers points out in *Room for Maneuver*, oppositional behavior "cannot—and does not attempt to—change the structure of power in which it operates... it merely exploits that structure of power for purposes of its own"(11). Though Achebe's intentions may differ, his earliest fiction is not a marked departure from that of the colonizers and their literary sponsors. For, having unwittingly bowed to the powerful propaganda of the invader (by rewriting the history of his people from the standpoint of the imperialists and lending their views substantial confirmation), Achebe can be said to have implemented, especially in his first novel, the very agendas he probably disdains and might have wanted to combat. Achebe's fiction allows the critic to measure the extent to which an assimilated writer from a dominated culture can escape the tyranny of his own upbringing, his conditioning, his (mis)education. This is part of the "politics of experience." There were subconscious pressures on Achebe's writing, created by his training as a native informant, a member of the Western educated elite. He did not have a free hand, an uninhibited freedom, to think through his earliest material, and to write without the implacable control of his immediate European predecessors.

Despite, no doubt, good intentions, Achebe's earliest creative writing relied upon forms that undermined some of his intentions, which serves as an example of how a cultural model imported from the imperial center can be an ineffective tool for attaining liberation. This work, then, offers an opportunity to meditate openly on the difficulty of resisting processes of acculturation as well as the problem criticism faces in trying to determine whether a writer's intentions have emerged as completely achieved in the work. The problem of how to handle influences shows up in the difficulty an author has in choosing whether to dismiss or highlight his milieu, and the critic must take that into account. We must resist, however, a trap into which many of Achebe's previous critics too often have fallen victim—that is, the tendency to equate the author's aesthetic intentions as spelled out in interviews, essays, and symposia with the actual creative accomplishment. Instead, we must look at his work itself with depth, insight, and detachment to evaluate the documentary truth Achebe has provided about his people as they undergo a major upheaval.

That Achebe never really found a way to get around dealing with the crisis of colonialism does not mean that no writer from the formerly colonized territory could do so. There is often a discrepancy between an author's intentions and actual achievement. Because this is true, readers of African literature must attend to not only the issue of cultural assertion but also the problems faced by African writers who attempt to work within conventional Western literary forms.[7] These problems are not limited to the "crisis of representation," the debilitating consciousness of the insufficiency of words, images, symbols, and concepts to capture the true essence of experience. African writers must also grapple with the reality of working with foreign languages—English in the case of Achebe. They also must confront Western forms such as the novel, poetry, drama, tragedy, satire, which have been used to silence indigenous voices. With these obstacles in mind, Achebe's success—however limited—with his first novel, *Things Fall Apart*, published in 1958, must be appreciated. It was one of the first major literary works by an African writer to deal with a specific imperial experience. He saw his role here, in *Things Fall Apart*, as rectifying the misrepresentation of the Igbos by the colonialists. He also tackled the job of showing that the colonists did not introduce the rule of law in the African colonies. Subsequent writers have not had to confront that issue, and could then focus on learning from the mistakes Achebe inevitably made in his use of Western forms. This is in accord with Eliot's idea in his classic essay "Tradition and the Individual Talent"; there is a realignment of values, structures, relations, and proportions in works of art whenever a new masterpiece is produced. While Achebe's stature and influence is deserved, African writers who have come after him have tried to learn from his errors. We can never read Achebe in the same way after the publication of these later works. In this way, "the past [can] be altered by the present" as Eliot claims ("Tradition," 50). Because each new era has needs that require changes in literary methods, the majority of post-*Things Fall Apart* experiments in the African novel have tended to put them in a class of their own. Many of these works aspire more to make global, post-independence statements (consider, for example, Wole Soyinka's *The Interpreters* and Ahmadu Kourouma's *The Suns of Independence*), than a localized statement.[9]

Among novels that deal with "identity reconstruction" or "cultural assertion," *Things Fall Apart* is archetypal. With its anthropological descriptiveness, its utilization of tribal turns of phrase and expression, and its goals of asserting the worth of African ways of life, it established a precedence. Set in a cluster of Igbo villages known as Umofia immediately before colonization, *Things Fall Apart* evokes the mood of tribal life by portraying ceremonies such as wrestling matches, religious rituals, festivals, weddings, and funerals, as well as the administration of justice. Through the involvement of the hero, Okonkwo, in both the public and private realms of life, Achebe recreates the complexity and charm of tribal life before colonization caused its decline. By emphasizing the way the Igbos accept each other as human beings with rights to express and uphold independent opinions, for example, he establishes their humanity in bold face.

Many African writers have been influenced by *Things Fall Apart* in particular and by *Arrow of God* to a lesser extent, although some have decided to avoid Achebe's mistakes, especially those of his first novel. One of the most valuable gifts that many younger writers have received from Achebe is his role of the writer as teacher. Achebe said that the writer who wanted to be a teacher must create exemplary characters in his/her fiction, but he never fully put his own ideas into practice. That has been one of the enigmas of his career. Why did Achebe leave room for writers like Ngugi, Iyayi, Ousmane (and others who followed) to test the possibilities of such a durable idea? One of the major contradictions in his fiction has been that Achebe wanted to preserve the values of his people but allowed the staunchest defenders of tradition the vulnerability they suffer. "Why does Okonkwo end tragically?" Arlene Elder asks in a recent study of *Things Fall Apart*. "This question haunts every reader of *Things Fall Apart*," she adds, "for we sense that a satisfactory answer would explain not only Chinua Achebe's complex protagonist but also the writer's larger concern about the destruction of traditional African society during the period of colonization."[10] Satisfactory reasons have never been offered for these perceived flaws, nor have viable solutions that could have led him out of the impasse been provided. The answer lies in his attitude toward imported Western literary models, especially his unwary dependence upon the conventions of tragedy.

The tragic mode contains qualities that limit its effectiveness as a method of realistic portraiture, for capturing life in its raw form. A. D. Nuttall's recent study *Why Does Tragedy Give Pleasure?* (1996) helps us understand why Achebe's goal was so severely hampered when he chose the tragic mode to express the experience of colonial conquest and domination. Whatever attractive literary qualities it may possess, tragedy gives pleasure (and thus is acquiescent) because we know it is a denial of reality. Tragedy gives pleasure rather than genuine pain in part because it is a self-indulgent form, a formalistic exercise that is often an end in itself.

Its impact depends on its ability to underscore the audience's "implicit awareness that what [it] is looking at is a representation, and not the thing itself" (83). Nuttall cites the case of the dramatist who may be "straining, within the mimesis, for an uncompromising despair" while at the same time attempting to "preserve a scrupulous loyalty to certain satisfying laws of form, which, if they do not compromise the despair, serve in the long run to mitigate it, which is almost the same thing" (83). Visiting the history of the form from antiquity, Nuttall comments,

> Ever since Aristotle pointed out that the emotions felt in the theatre are hypothetical rather than categorical—that is, that we weep at the thought of what would happen rather than at an actual disaster—the pleasure of tragedy has been linked to its palpable unreality; for the hypothetical, unlike the categorical, is within our control, and our secure sovereignity is manifested in the stately artistic form we confer upon it. (Nuttal, *Why Does Tragedy Give Pleasure?*)[11]

Tragedy is a totalizing convention with the capacity to neatly package character, plot, symbolism, and language. Many younger African writers have broken away from the tradition, conscious of its repressive tendencies, its formalism, its unreality, its legitimization of hegemony.

These late writers seek to authorize the voices of the powerless by challenging traditional discourses of power. They create a more compelling portrait of colonization, because they rely upon less imperial, less simulated, less majestic modes. They turn narratives of oppression into epics of liberation, creating a revamped vision of order that restores faith in the people's ability to take linguistic and political control of their own destiny. I am thinking in particular of Buchi Emecheta (*The Rape of Shavi*), Festus Iyayi (*Heroes*) and Ngugi wa Thiong'o (*A Grain of Wheat* and *Petals of Blood*).

Haunted and stung by Okonkwo's (and his people's) defeat, these younger writers have chosen to revise Achebe's bleak view of African history. By progressing from defeat to victory in their works, talented writers such as Iyayi, Omotoso, Emecheta, and Ngugi, to cite only a few examples, have made major contributions toward radicalizing the African novel. They call into question the old notion of "history" as an elitist narrative, and innovatively discard the ideological timidity restraining the range of characters whose experiences have been considered pivotal to fiction; they create experimental works that make radical uses of oral narrative.

These younger writers seek to build an ordered world out of the disorder imposed first by colonialism and then, after political independence, by the indigenous elite. The turn away from the lofty narrative conventions associated with Achebe points to these authors' opposition to stories that seem to undermine the corporate will and confidence.[12]

Novels by the younger African writers have been written in response to Achebe's. Coming to these novels from Achebe's enables us to see how radical perspectives can make indigenous use of history. History, or the record of a people's achievements, ought to be about their whole way of life, the record of their past, from which their present condition has emerged. It also should be an account of the experiences from which a people's sense of future direction can be molded. History as grand narrative has been commonly rewritten by committed African writers dissatisfied with history as a record of elite experience. Revision is necessary because of the hold such narratives have on a community's self-definition.

Many committed African writers after Achebe have felt compelled to step outside history, using myth or portraying the past as it might have been, either to make a difficult present bearable or to create a more positive future. By modifying Achebe's conception of history, and by reconfiguring the genre of the African novel inaugurated by Achebe, these younger writers force a reconsideration of the value of history. They enjoin readers to understand that artistic commitment goes well beyond helping to repair the image of Africa damaged in the fiction of European writers, i.e., Achebe's notion of the duty of the African writer. They accept Achebe's idea of authentically portraying the history and culture of Africa, but they consider imaginative projection paramount. For the younger writers, the crucial issue is the role history can play redefining African identity. Rather than depicting history simplistically, or as an aristocratic tale, these younger writers aspire to create a popular tale that transcends a surface picture of events. They provide a deeper analysis of the underlying causes of history than Achebe did before them especially in his earliest work, although they do so, in part, by building on his achievement, both as a model and by transcending its limits.

This new conception of history is certainly crucial to the programs of self-rehabilitation pursued in Ngugi's *A Grain of Wheat* and *Petals of Blood*; Adaora Ulasi's *Many Thing You No Understand*; Sembene's *God's Bits of Wood*; Iyayi's *Heroes*, Nwapa's *One is Enough*; Sow Fall's *The Beggar's Strike*. To Achebe's credit, his novels were the first to offer biting criticism of the postcolonial era, in *No Longer at Ease*, *A Man of the People*, and *Anthills of the Savannah*. However, those coming after Achebe have taken this project to another level. *No Longer at Ease*, an archetypal work, that is, the founding text in this movement, seeks, for example, far less to examine the dilemma of an individual than that of a group, the Western-educated Africans and their cross-cultural predicament. With this novel, Achebe inspired others to write about the journey abroad. The journey in African literature involves both psychological and physical movement. In Mongo Beti's *Mission to Kala*, the growth in consciousness on the trip is revealed as no less demanding than the journey away from home. In *America, Their America*, J. P. Clark, an African student in America, records the dehumanizing effects of racism.[13] In a seminal contribution, Achebe made the African novel of the journey a study in irony: The retreat to what the journey-maker hopes will be a sanctuary often turns into a site of bitter disappointment and extreme disillusionment. In works similar to *No Longer at Ease*, such novels as Armah's *Fragments* and *Why Are We So Blest?* or Kourouma's *Les Soliels des independences*), a protagonist who returns from abroad sees anew the oppression and injustice that emanate from maladministration in post-colonial Africa. Confronted with the betrayal of the dream of independence, the writers blame the crises on the rulers' unpatriotic attitude. While the younger authors propose creative writing as a fighting role for themselves, one similar to Achebe's (to put an end to the massive political improbity on the continent), their artistic achievements are incongruent in terms of narrative design and structure, the use of setting, symbolism, characters, and satire. Although much of the works of the younger writers retains some of Achebe's somber tone, they offer a more positive picture of Africa than Achebe did in his bleak text.[14]

In his first novel, Achebe began with the idea of social relevance, a means of bearing witness to imperial domination. Although Achebe in his early novels, covering the nascent and last phases of colonialism, unavoidably adopted the posture of an ardent celebrant of tradition, the dilemma he faced was how to bear witness to colonialism without seeing and presenting his observations through the lenses of the European detractors. The sustained glance into the past taken by such later writers as Soyinka, Ngugi, Laye, Beti, Omotoso, Emecheta, and Awoonor is part of their attempt to improve upon Achebe's work. They do not think he was entirely successful in simultaneously documenting traditional African customs, values, attitudes, and behaviors while recording the dehumanizing effects of colonialism. Achebe's primary early goal was to extrapolate from history motifs, ideas, and values that typified the precolonial African way of life; but the younger writers find the old forms, such as proverbs, riddles, and tragedy favored by Achebe, inadequate for dealing with contemporary social problems. They have searched for artistic forms that could better represent the new realities (like the folktale in Ngugi's *Matigari*) and describe women's experiences (like Buchi Emecheta's *The Rape of Shavi*), which were missing in earlier patriarchal works.

To be sure, the impetus to end oppression and to create an ideal social order does not guarantee artistically satisfying literature. It may lead to programatic imprudence, as in Ayi Kwei Armah's *The Healers* and Achebe's *Anthills of the Savannah*. This notwithstanding, *Anthills of the Savannah* is significant for its experimentation with the new aesthetics of liberation. Both in form and ideology, *Anthills* marks a major departure for Achebe. This passionate attempt to unite history and myth suggests that this departure came from Achebe's own deeply felt convictions as well as the pull of the work of the younger writers. Recent events had also called into question the very adequacy of the old forms he had used as a writer. We need to investigate carefully the sources and the results of the search that Achebe is making to come to grips with new forms of expression. What new visions of Africa, for example, have resulted from Achebe's new art, and what contribution do they make to the genre of the African novel? How should one respond to critics' almost unanimous praise for *Anthills of the Savannah*? Is *Anthills* as flawless as it has been made out to be? [15]

Having too great an expectation of Achebe can surely lead those who think it doesn't fit the artistic mode they have come to associate with him to consider the novel a disappointment. It could well be argued, for example, that the urgency of the message he wishes to put across appears so pressing that considerations of plot or the well-made story, probability, and development of character and logic have become relatively inconsequential. Since a work of high formal harmony is what many readers have come to expect from Achebe, that would be a disappointing regression.

Anthills of the Savannah initially seems as though it begins without any clear sense of direction, displaying all through its pages numerous aimless dialogues, some uninspiring and bland descriptive passages, as well as awkward characterization. Examples include the poorly written "Hymn to the Sun," the aimless scene featuring the car race, the overly detailed descriptions of the food and drinks served at the party held at the presidential retreat, the purposeless description in Beatrice's lengthy monologue, the inconsistent and melodramatic characterization of Chris. If judged by the conventional rules of European realist fiction, *Anthills of the Savannah* has been unable to impose a richness of narrative structure whose texture and range meet our expectations. Things like particularity of time, place, and characterization are not harmoniously integrated.

Such an impression may be due more to the reader's failure to respond to this truly new work, which appears to have absorbed elements from the hitherto spurned tradition of the thriller. The strictures derive far more from the incapacity to appreciate the new formal structure within which Achebe is working than from any intrinsic compositional weaknesses. It can be argued that the redemptive sight that propels the action more than compensates for some of the dissappointing formal elements in Achebe's latest novel. To fully appreciate Achebe's accomplishment in that work, readers must be cognizant of the new revolution that has occurred in African writing, whereby the impulse to pry open the wounds of the present has been necessitated by the desire not only to establish a logical link between the past and the future in an ugly chain of events but also to tame the tide of disorder in the continent using fresh narrative frames. *Anthill* belongs firmly in this new culture. Though questions inevitably will arise as to this novel's artistic merit, *Anthills* calls into question the accepted dividing lines between art and politics, signalling the radical ideological transformation that has occurred in Achebe's approach to the novel.

Achebe's work must be placed in perspective, that is, within the context of Europe's encounter with Africa, and his determination to be a guiding light in our quest to understand the ramifications of colonialism. Literature was one of the weapons that the British used not only to justify but to enhance the colonization project. Thus, all through the writings of European explorers and settlers, Africans had been treated as creatures living in an infantile state within environments filled with disease, squalor, and degradation that ostensibly legitimized the colonization intended to bring about improvement of the African. The crusade to eliminate the lingering ideas of Africans' innate inferiority was the greatest challenge that pioneering African writers like Achebe felt called upon to tackle. Especially in his novels, Achebe tries to go considerably beyond the scope and contours of a colonial text in his account of the African's personality. However, it is unfortunate that, much as he has tried, Achebe could not entirely avoid duplicating some of the images of Africans promoted by colonialist literature, because he over-relied on their narrative conventions. Not until a second generation of indigenous writers appeared did African writing undergo a profound change, both in its attempt to reverse the image of the African and in the originality of the idioms employed in that exploration. However, to understand the significance of this shift, one must first consider the pioneering role of Chinua Achebe.

Chapter 2

THE COLONIAL OCCUPATION

"Although generalizations are of course dangerous," V. Y. Mudimbe writes in his widely acclaimed book *The Invention of Africa*, "*colonialism* and *colonization* basically mean organization and arrangement."[1] Mudimbe could start out his study with such an astonishing statement because he initially seeks the meanings of colonialism and colonization through theory, an abstraction, encoded in the Latin words "colere, meaning to cultivate or to design." If Mudimbe, thus, leaves his readers to wonder what happened to the unprecedented reign of terror, the hardship and confusion, the unimaginable suffering unleashed by colonization, what are we to make of Achebe, who, without such a philosophical cast of mind, also decides not to acknowledge immediately that colonization involved real human victims?[2] Achebe's *Things Fall Apart* was the foundation of modern African literature. He is responsible for adopting an acquiescient attitude instead of trying to define the holocaust of colonization. Nevertheless, Achebe himself recognizes that he began his writing career from the position of acute cultural and moral ambivalence.

In his recent essay, "African Literature as Restoration of Celebration," Achebe admits that he has been unable to disengage completely from the cleavages of a colonial education:

> I went to a good school modelled on British public schools. I read lots of English books there. I read *Treasure Island* and *Gulliver's Travels* and *Prisoner of Zenda*, and *Oliver Twist* and *Tom Brown's School Days* and such books in their dozens. But I also encountered Ryder Haggard and John Buchan and the rest, and their 'African' books. *I did not see myself as an African to begin with. I took sides with*

> *the white men against the savages. In other words I went through my first level of school thinking I was of the party of the white man in his hair-raising adventures and narrow escapes. The white man was good and reasonable and intelligent and courageous. The savages arrayed against him were sinister and stupid or, at the most, cunning. I hated their guts,* (emphasis added).[3]

Though he may have changed his feelings since those days, there is ambivalence in his fiction that is a result of his colonial education. Afterall, he wrote his first novel while a school boy at the university college at Ibadan. This conflict has remained with him since the nearly forty years after his undergraduate studies; Achebe could still recall the diet of the English writers' works he had been fed in college. This suggests the implacable hold those works undoubtedly have exercised, and no doubt continue to exercise, on his imagination.

In accord with the literary legacy upon which Achebe has drawn for the construction of *Things Fall Apart*, my discussion of the novel begins with the physiological attributes associated with the work's hero. As Okonkwo Unoka begins the quest for a distinctive career in Igbo society, Achebe describes his spectacular athletic achievements and then his physical appearance, and finally his mental make-up, which is said to be dominated by emotion. The relevant part reads as follows:

> He was tall and huge, and his bushy eyebrows and wide nose gave him a very severe look. He breathed heavily, and it was said that, when he slept, his wives and children in their out-houses could hear him breathe. When he walked, his heels hardly touched the ground and he seemed to walk on springs, as if he was going to pounce on somebody. And he did pounce on people quite often. He had a slight stammer and whenever he was angry and could not get his words out quickly enough, he would use his fists. He had no patience with unsuccessful men. He had no patience with his father.[4]

Surely one of the arresting qualities of this passage is the peculiar conceptualization of this character's identity, which conforms to the depiction of the personality of the savage in the colonial novel of Africa stretching from the works of Cary and Conrad to that of Greene. Achebe's influence is clearly the English literary tradition, which portrays Africans as barbaric.

In the European novel about Africa, the African character is invariably depicted to show his essential difference from the European norm. Achebe's text can be said to have absorbed this tradition since it juxtaposes such peculiar traits as the "bushy eyebrows and wide nose" and emotionality commonly associated with the primitive Africans with European reason and logic. Okonkwo is painted as if he lacks the ordinary gift of articulate human speech in a way that is too close to the Conradian image of Africans without a human voice. Thus, predictably, throughout the text, Okonkwo is presented as an overgrown child, whose story details the movement of a typical European pastoral tragedy. In works of this tradition the country confronts the city and the defender of the status quo such as Michael Henchard, who resists change in Thomas Hardy's *The Mayor of Casterbridge*, is swept away by it. The dominant idea in pastoral themes is the inevitable victory of the complex urban civilization over a simple and innocent rural life, with tragic consequences for "the self-alienated" man. In *Things Fall Apart*, Western influence equates nicely with the complex metropolitan urban life-style that the hero, Okonkwo, standing for simple African ways, resists at his own peril. This is why the novel gives emphasis to the fact that Okonkwo has all but overcome the poverty and lowly status inherited from his birth, when the white man arrives and incites the enemy within, i.e., fear of failure and of being thought weak, which leads him into a pattern of disruptive behavior that results in his breaking societal taboos. When he moves from severity toward his children to wife-beating and attempted murder, then cuts down Ikemefuna, his foster child, before he finally commits the homicide that leads him into his suicide, Okonkwo proves unable to conquer this opponent, the enemy within.

The reason and balance exhibited by Okonkwo's greatest friend Obierika and his uncle Uchendu exist as counterweights, but his effort to go beyond the generic image of Africans is not entirely successful. Achebe accepts the modes of discourse dictated by the European novel of Africa rather than rejecting them. While the profiles of Obierika and Uchendu may be significant for the reveal-

17

ing light they throw on the novel's main protagonist, the ability of the Europeans to hoodwink the Africans shows after all that Achebe's story is not all that different from that told, say, in any of the Captain W. E Johns' Biggle narratives, where Africans are usually presented as duped savages. Other Africans—in the story interpreters and court messengers—depict Africans in light which shows them as all too willing to kill for cheap trinkets. This is the pattern of depiction that stems from Conrad's *Heart of Darkness*.

Achebe is caught up in such European games of duality as the trite contrasts of white and black, Europe and Africa, good and evil, reason and emotion, and similar other simple-minded binary oppositions. Because many readers go to the African novel expecting some level of factual account of historical events, it is unfortunate that *Things Fall Apart* not only has perpetuated such stereotypes, but has taken some pleasure in treating the atrocities of colonialism with levity , going so far as to offer justification for their occurrence.

Things Fall Apart can be located within the tradition of the European colonial African novel. We need to scrutinize the view of colonization depicted within its pages, instead of being over-awed by its linguistic power (as have commentators such as R. N. Egudu, Simon Gikandi, David Carroll, G. D. Killam, and Eustace Palmer) or by its use of proverbs for conveying the African's cast of mind (Bernth Lindfors, C. L. Innes, Nwachukwu-Agbada, Emmanuel Obiechina, and Donatus Nwoga); or by its ability to employ culture to showcase the fundamental worth of the African as a human being (Hunt Hawkins, Donatus Nwoga, Dan Izevbaye, Oladele Taiwo, and Robert Wren).

There is no need to recycle continually the view that *Things Fall Apart* offers a slice of traditional life in a compelling and evocative language. From its opening pages it is indeed powerfully crisp in its descriptive passages of a human society in full splendor. It clearly depicts noteworthy qualities of African tribal society, such as the Igbo respect for life, the corporate good of the group, and the esteem for personal achievement, which permeates African society. Furthermore, that the Igbo culture has a lively and throbbing vigor seems to serve the author well as a means of disproving some of the claims of colonialist writers like Conrad, Cary, and Haggard—all of whom dismiss Africans as quaint and barbaric. Indeed, overall, nothing can better drive home the merits of Igbo civilization's regard for feminine principles that protect the weak from the strong than the eventual ruin of Okonkwo, who falls from the heights as a result of his relentless struggle to supress his own feminine qualities.

Despite the significance of the theme of cultural assertion, Achebe insists that his more important objective is to demonstrate the way in which the coming of the white man was a decisive factor in fragmenting tribal ways. In *Things Fall Apart*, whites arrive in Igboland shortly after Okonkwo is expelled from Umofia, although it is not until his second year in exile that readers discover much about it. The sudden appearance of the white man becomes one of the major events, its unfolding revealed primarily in relation to Okonkwo's reaction. It is one of the most egregious problems that he will encounter in all of his career. Occasioning the white presence just at a time that Okonkwo is about to score a major triumph serves as an effective way to rouse him to a new level of uncertainty. It also heightens the reader's curiosity as to what Okonkwo will make of his life in exile.

Okonkwo's friend Obierika, the prime bearer of the news, appropriately relates it with virtuosity. By employing specificity of locale, he advances the credibility of the tale. Obierika casts the narrative in such a manner that it draws its appeal as much from what he leaves unexplained as from what he includes. The state of unpreparedness in which the sudden appearance of the British catches the unsuspecting people of Abame is emphasized to lend a tragic aura to their inability to cope with it. The timing of the occurrence is crucial because it compares them with the arrival of pests. It occurs during the planting season. The innocent people of Abame spot a strange object riding "an iron horse" (a bicycle), and, fearing for their lives, the elders consult their oracle, who warns that the intruder will "break the clan and spread destruction among them." Significantly, the oracle adds that "other white men were on their way. They were locusts, it said, and that first man was their harbinger sent to explore the terrain."[5]

Because even the oracles themselves do not appear to have been able to do anything more than give warning, what we have is the standard stuff out of which tragedy is made. The narrative lets the people reason that they could act in self-defense by putting the white man to death, after which they tie his bicycle to their sacred silk cotton tree, so it would not "run away to call the man's friends." Predictably, by so doing, the villagers expose their community to the merciless retributive anger and violence of the white colonizers, who, like a flash of lightning, send an army composed of white officers and black servicemen to pounce on the village during a market day, when the people least suspected an invasion. The attempt at self-defense brings the villagers speedily into an encounter with a dreaded fate.

Obierika attempts to stress the swiftness and thoroughness of the attack. Like all anecdotes, Obierika's story may stand for a bigger story, since it primarily employs an evocative style loaded with grave significations. By the very nature of its telling, the story also reveals the author's awareness of how issues of military violence and power, how stories told about the confrontation between native peoples and the colonial invaders are to be recounted or processed for the consumption of his primary audience of readers based in Europe and America. The novelist's own reaction to the brutality of the occupation forces is not exposed, and Obierika's account excludes the gory details of the attack, which suggests that the attack was not without some justification.

Okonkwo's peace-loving uncle Uchendu blames the people of Abame for bringing doom upon themselves, because they murdered a stranger who did not say an offensive word, something that violates Igbo tradition. Okonkwo, himself, also places the blame on the people, but for a different reason. "'They were fools,' said Okonkwo after a pause.' They had been warned that danger was ahead. They should have armed themselves with their guns and their matchets even when they went to market'."[6] He concludes, angrily, that the Abame people were weak and foolish. Obierika shares the fear aroused by "stories of white men who made the powerful guns and strong drinks and took slaves away across the seas, but no one thought the stories were true."[7]

Through the chilling silence and neutrality of tone he maintains, the author of *Things Fall Apart* panders to the taste of his metropolitan (European) audience. This is part of the cultural politics of narration. It is now commonly agreed by most historians (Afigbo, Anene, Ekechi, Isichei) that the story told by Obierika is not entirely fictitious; that, in fact, the fictional attack on Abame is not

Achebe's invention but is based substantially on a massacre that occurred in Ahiara in 1905. The story is based on the retaliation by the British for the murder of a certain Dr. Stewart, which led to intensification of the British use of force in colonizing the Bende-Onitsha hinterland and beyond. Achebe's failure to give his reaction to the horror of the event is not all that different from the attitude of any British officer who observes the same event from a discrete distance.[8]

Readers who didn't know enough about the role that military violence played in the pacification of Igboland will learn little from the picture emerging from this novel, which emphasizes the humanitarianism that ostensibly accompanied the British "civilizing mission." In her book *The Ibo People and the Europeans*, Elizabeth Isichei, a New Zealander married to an Igbo, stresses that the Igbo did not welcome the Europeans with open arms, but resisted them with full force. In this they were unlike other Nigerian peoples who are located within the submissive Northern Emirate.[9] It is because of this resistance—not arising from an unsuspectingly tranquil people—that "salutary displays of superior force" were brought to bear on the Igbo to demonstrate the futility of any attempt to resist.

In another study, *A History of the Ibo People*, Isichei maintains that the execution of what was seen as retributive justice by the British forces was not only high-handed but arbitrary, lawless, and incongruous. For, whereas the colonizers regarded "the death of a single European, at the hands of those whose country was being conquered by his compatriots [as] a brutal murder," they callously saw the death of hundreds of Igbos defending their native land with basic implements like matchets and muzzle loaders in the face of machine fire as "a good bag of the enemy."[10] That the British occupation of Igboland was attended by violence, and that the action of the people of Abame/Ahiara is clear demonstration of how resistance to colonization was common among the Igbo should have been a central concern in a supposedly history based work like *Things Fall Apart*.

Why is Achebe silent on the subject of violence and armed resistance, when he clearly recognizes that "stories are not innocent... they can be used to put you in the wrong crowd, in the party of the man who has come to dispossess you"?[11] Is he taken in by tragedy's fascination with the colorful and the innocent? The exiled West Indian novelist V. S. Naipul who lives and writes in England, said in 1971 that African novelists who wanted to get published during the early stages of African writing had to amuse, impress, and write for the European world.[12] It is more likely the case that Achebe was doing what was necessary to be published than that he was naive.

Inasmuch as present-day readers go to Achebe's novels searching for both values and meaning as well as for historical information, it is particularly troubling that the earliest meeting between the Igbo and the British, which was marked with so much blood, is lightly dismissed in the casual story narrated by Obierika. Instead of giving an incident many consider paradigmatic of the conquest of all Africa a mere anecdotal space, he ought to have highlighted with depth and feeling the far-reaching consequencies of the British attack and the resistance of the Igbo people. The projection of the novelist's expressed belief that the subsequent benefits of the colonizing mission justify the colonization project as a whole reveals poor judgment on his part as well. An opportunity was missed to use the Abame episode to demonstrate clearly and decisively not only the fact of British absolute superiority in arms, but also of the sense of the extreme cruelty that the British showed in their response to the resistance that Africans demonstrated against forces seeking to conquer them.

In *Resistance Literature* Barbara Harlow writes eloquently about the power of narrative within the context of third world liberation,

> The historical struggle against colonialism and imperialism of such resistance movements as the PLO (Palestine),the FLN (Algeria), the NLF (Vietnam), Mau Mau (Kenya), FRELIMO (Mozambique), BPLF (Baluchistan), the ANC (South Africa), FREITLIN (East Timor), the FMLN (El Salvador), or the Sandinista FSLN (Nicaragua), and whether successful in their struggle as yet or not, is waged at the same time as a struggle over the historical or cultural record... The struggle over the historical record is seen as no less crucial than the armed struggle.[13]

Because voice is such an effective weapon for attaining freedom from domination, nothing has been more contentious than the
power to shape and control its contours. The omission by *Things
Fall Apart* to delineate the aftereffects of colonization accurately
has genuine, yet terrible importance. We can hold it partly responsible for the gap that currently exists in Nigerian literary history and
the denials and silences about the divisions caused among Africans, because Nigerian literary history in its wake has revealed
nothing but a tragic sense of misplaced priorities. Whereas the Nigeria-Biafra War of 1967-1970, which followed in the wake of independence, has produced more than twenty novels by writers of
Igbo origin alone, not a single Nigerian novelist has documented
vividly the resistance to the British conquest, though it was the
original cause of the Biafran War.[14] What this means is that, by his
initial act of omission, Achebe unwittingly contributed to the image
of Africans as their own worst enemies, who continue to fight among
themselves after gaining self-rule, and who have been unable to
govern themselves capably. Had he shown a different example,
other writers would undoubtedly have followed his lead.

In regard to *Things Fall Apart*, when one considers that the
ideology of an author is revealed as much by what he suppresses
as by what he includes, one can see how much Achebe has undermined his own role of teacher. Of course, Achebe did not invent
the notion of relative peacefulness of the take-over of Igboland:
British propaganda did. Achebe simply confirms it by deflecting
attention away from the violence that attended the British arrival.
The irony is that Achebe has denounced writers like Joseph Conrad,
who effaced the African's humanity; yet, in *Things Fall Apart*, he
fell into another form of lop-sidedness by failing to give proportion-
ate attention to the uproar that accompanied colonization, which in
due time involved returning fire with fire.[15]

Achebe criticized Joseph Conrad's *Heart of Darkness* for call-
ing "the humanity of African people into question."[16] However, in
Things Fall Apart Achebe himself portrays Africans with an almost identical treatment. This puzzle is clarified in the interview
with Nwachukwu-Agbada, where Achebe confesses to having internalized all of the imperialist assumptions about Africa. At the
time he wrote his first novel, Achebe had not yet weaned himself
from his schooling in Western ideas about Africa.[17]

The fact that *Things Fall Apart* utilizes the authority of liberalism accounts for the great fascination it holds, especially for Western audiences, who see in it not only confirmation of their own preconceptions about Africa but also a work that projects familiar images of Africa in its use of European narrative conventions. If Western readers such as Florence Stratton have commonly regarded it as "the most important work by an African writer," it is because *Things Fall Apart* is a paean to the triumph of colonialism and the success of European cultural imperialism.[18] Stratton, one of many who rate it highly, further states that "Over five-million copies of the book have been sold and it has been translated into thirty languages. Its influence on the development of the contemporary African literary and critical tradition has been substantial."[19] Sales figures may not be the best way to assess the value of a work of art, but they indicate that conforming to stereotyped views such as the notion of African submissiveness and closesness to nature and African primitivism can win millions of friendly readers in colonial centers.

However much influence it might possess, *Things Fall Apart* nevertheless belongs in the category of those curious works of the intellect Benedict Anderson in *Imagined Communities* has associated with the pathology of colonization.[20] In Anderson's view, this is manifested in an artist's tendency to show blind love for the nation even when the nation is often itself an artificial creation of colonialism. What is ironic, as Anderson appropriately maintains, is "how truly rare it is to find *analogous* nationalist products expressing fear and loathing" since "[e]ven in the case of colonized peoples, who have every reason to feel hatred for their imperialist rulers, it is astonishing how insignificant the element of hatred is in these expression of national feeling."[21] Although Anderson does not specifically mention *Things Fall Apart* in his study, it clearly belongs in the tradition of writings by former colonized peoples characterized by Anderson as betraying significant clues pointing to self-contempt.

One of the most demeaning features of the novel is surely the derisive laughter, which is aimed by the author at caricaturing the local people who serve as informants for the missionaries, who are themselves glamourized. The curiosity of this attitude is that much of the perverted love shown for the outsiders contains a corre-

sponding quality of self-disdain. That the missionaries are vener-
ated is indicated by their being called by honorific titles such as Mr.
Brown and Mr. Smith. A similar honor is denied local converts
such as Enoch and Moses Unachukwu as well as to every traditionalist featured in the novel. Not even the protagonist, Okonkwo,
nor elders like Obierika, Akunna, and Uchendu, have been left out
of this politics of naming. Black interpreters, colonial police personnel, and court messengers are depicted in a comic light instead of
with an emphasis on their role in the execution of colonial policies.
They are presented, not in intimate detail, but only in functionalist
terms, which minimalizes their humanity. Such a technique may not
necessarily imply a weakness of representation, but the use of these
characters, portrayed as a bunch of idiots, as objects of ridiculous
laughter for the entertainment of readers, is an approach that oversimplifies excessively. Intelligent, sneaky, street-wise, these
middlmen believe they can outwit the Europeans because, although
originally employed by the Europeans to serve as tools for facilitat-
ing colonization, they have turned their positions to self-serving ends.

The unexpected fracas that takes place when Enoch's action of
unmasking an *egwungwun*, one of the titled elders sent to settle
the land dispute with the missionaries, resulting in Enoch's home
being burned down by the villagers, we may sense that the interpreter who accompanies the white officer sent to negotiate the
crisis is actually enjoying himself, taking undue liberties that do anything but quel the crisis. The villagers know that, without the back-
ing of the missionaries, Enoch could not have defiled their tradition
so brazenly, that is, by killing and eating the sacred royal python.
Since Enoch is only a fanatic who acts out a lessson he has been
taught by the missionaries, the group of elders traditionally charged
with the administration of justice in the community, the *egwungwun*,
appropriately directs their anger at Rev. Smith. This is how the
performance of the interpreter Josiah Okeke is described when the
egwungwun go to the church to confront Rev. Smith:

> Ajofia. . . . the leading *egwungwun* of Umofia . . . .addressed
> Mr. Smith . . . "Tell the white man that we will not do him any
> harm," he said to the interpreter. "Tell him to go back to his
> house and leave us alone. We liked his brother who was
> with us before . . . . But this shrine which he built must be

> destroyed. We shall no longer allow it in our midst. It has
> bred untold abominations and we have come to put an end
> to it . . . ."
>
> Mr. Smith said to his interpreter: "Tell them to go away
> from here. This is the house of God and I will not live to see
> it desecrated."
>
> Okeke interpreted wisely to the spirits and leaders of
> Umofia: "The white man says he is happy you have come
> to him with your grievances, like friends. He will be happy if
> you leave the matter in his hands."[22]

Though the devious interpreter thinks that the blatant lie he tells is funny, the opposite is true. Okeke's cunning does not prevent the destruction of this particular church; and it achieves something far worse: It "saves the Reverend from paying too high a price for his candor."[23] By tempering the tenor of Reverend Smith's hostile statement, the interpreter alters the character of communication between the agent of the conqueror and the subjugated people. This action prevents the native people from getting to know the truth about the utter contempt in which they are held by the missionaries. Had it been made clear to the villagers that the white man did not consider himself to be a visitor but as one who has come to take full control over the land and the people, it is doubtful that anything could have prevented an intensification of resistance by the local people.

In return for his services on behalf of colonization, what does the interpreter receive? The missionaries tossed perks to him, items that include shares from the livestock and other gifts that habitually go with the hospitality the natives customarily extended to the interpreters whenever they had doubled as policemen. The native informant really could be said to have sold not only his soul but also his inheritance for a mess of pottage and for a life of luxury.

Things Fall Apart presents these go-betweens as outsiders, some of them the offspring of freed slaves who had gained early exposure to Western influences. Because of this comic fun can be made of their dialect and comportment. The middlemen are so strategic to pacification that the novel attributes to them the final blow that causes the destruction of the old order: It is Okonkwo's killing of the messenger which leads to his suicide. Curiously enough, in this novel we never really see anyone except Okonkwo take a serious attitude toward these middlemen either individually or as a group.

Sketching the interpreter as vain and vulgar, and as being inclined to the peccadilloes of cheating and joyous contentment, is typical of the way white conquerors depict a subject people. The image of the comic foreign black servant painted to show his difference from the true Igbo norm for the entertainment of the oppressor recalls the manner of the Irish writers who perpetrated the stereotype of themselves painted by English authors at the time of Ireland's greatest persecution.[24] To write in this humorous way about the painful dilemma of these human beings is to write derisively. While in any situation of this nature there may be bound to exist a comic aspect, a writer who exercises his liberty to dwell solely and unduly on the merriment he derives from his observation of such incidents simply opens himself to the charge of alienation.

Furthermore, the missionaries are divided into two categories— good or bad—which makes it difficult to perceive that they all represent the same message, despite differences in personality. Acculturation of the native is the goal of that message; practiced intimidation, the vehicle for its delivery. That not even a man as reputable as Obierika could escape the effect of such intimidation shows the power of the weapon of the missionaries. The indirect tribute paid the British by Obierika demonstrates the fawning, beggarly attitude to which he is reduced. According to Obierika, as he tells the story of the roots of colonization, military violence went hand-in-hand with mental conditioning to make the conquest: "The missionaries had come to Umofia. They had built their church there, won a handful of converts and were already sending evangelists to the surrounding towns and villages."[25]

The missionaries capitalize upon the opportunity available to them in Igboland. The number of converts is an index of their effectiveness. Since Obierika's visit to Mbanta, the place of Okonkwo's exile, is itself prompted by his need to commiserate with his friend over the conversion of one of his sons, it is appropriate that Obierika emphasize the commanding presence of the new forces. Although chance also played a role, the success of imperial conquest is largely because of the white man's ability to use the natives as tools for colonizing the hinterland. Since he himself did not speak the Igbo language, he depended on the voice of the faithful local informant, who in turn based a part of his ability to convert other natives on his privileged access to the local culture. Through the interpreter, the invader thus pushes his message, a large portion of it conveyed in sermons that reveal the burden that the missionaries believed they bore: the charge of delivering communities of unbelievers from damnation. By ending with the alleged instant infatuation the communities are believed to show with such products of Western technology as the bicycle, which the missionaries promise them not only to ride but also to own in abundance later, the text gives primacy to the subject of the material rewards that colonialism ostensibly used to unsettle the traditional order.[26]

Charging the duty of early pacification to Brown, a missionary described as being of kindly disposition, makes it particularly easier for the novel to sustain the notion that the proselytization of Igboland was peaceable and mutually beneficial to both the conqueror and the conquered. We are made to believe that Brown owed the success of his work primarily to the moderate approach he took for conversion. The friendship that Brown is considered to have established with the elders of the village was so great that: "Whenever Mr. Brown went to that village he spent long hours with Akunna in his *obi* talking through an interpreter about religion. Neither of them succeeded in converting the other but they learnt more about their different beliefs."[27] Much of what passes as Brown's success story, however, is hardly convincing, for how can a colonial officer, who has simply found a leisurely means for coping with boredom, succeed so well in deceiving the natives into believing that he genuinely values their conversation? In the character of Brown, there seems to be too much of the quality of Captain Cook, the figure in Polynesian history who Gananath Obeyesekere has called a mythical creation of the European imagination: "The European god... a new type of explorer... a great navigator, a decent human being, the man who described Polynesia and its peoples."[28] Brown may appear to be treading softly on the faith of the people, but he wears it down anyway. Brown is depicted as a good tactician, a man able to make the villagers believe that he is what he is not—their friend—even while he is silently causing the gradual disintegration of the world they cherish so dearly. Though Brown appears to be a liberal, in fact, he is a racist paternalist. Contrary to what he would have them believe, Brown does not really have much respect for the subjugated people. Since the author conceals his attitude toward Brown, his depiction represents the highest form of narrative improbability.

Mr. Smith, Brown's successor, though portrayed as evil, is also more a stereotype than a convincingly real person. Nevertheless, Smith's character is more in accord with the real history of conquest. Smith candidly states his purpose right away: to transform a primitive society in dire need of deliverance.

> Mr. Smith was greatly distressed by the ignorance which many of his flock showed even in such things as the Trinity and the sacraments. It only showed that they were seeds sown on a rocky soil. Mr. Brown had thought of nothing but numbers. He should have known that the kingdom of God did not depend on large crowds. Our Lord Himself stressed the importance of fewness. Narrow is the way and few the number. To fill the Lord's holy temple with an idolatrous crowd clamouring for signs was a folly of everlasting consequence. Our Lord used the whip only once in his life—to drive the crowd away from His church.[29]

This passage is significant. A remarkable instance of the successful use of the free indirect discourse, it provides an apt example of the informed Christian sermon, in which Smith tells things as he perceives them, up front, showing evidence of some form of honesty. But most critics who discuss the activities of the missionaries in *Things Fall Apart* overlook the importance of this element of candor, tending, instead, to concentrate on Smith's seemingly inflexible disposition. The exhaltation of diplomacy, however, which associates refinement with compassion but links candor with cruelty, ignores the crucial fact that all roads taken in the colonial enterprise lead to the same goal: the control of the mind, of the body, and of the space of the African, all resulting to his being diverted from his normal course of being.[30]

Okonkwo's son, Nwoye's conversion is one good example of the irretreivable loss that accompanies such control, yet it is not presented as a result of institutionalized violence directed against both his personal dignity and his community, but as the result of internal stresses within traditional African society. Nwoye's dis-

29

comfort with traditional society stems from the stories of masculine violence that his father told him, combined with his father's constant chastisement of him for being drawn to feminine roles. Is it possible that Nwoye never heard about the massacre at Abame? Or did Nwoye consider the murder of hundreds of people in that village less significant than the ritual execution of his friend and the predicament of twins occasionally left abandoned to die in the bush? Why is there so much emphasis on these infrequent practices and so little on the offenses of the colonialists?

From the standpoint of the narrative, Nwoye's turn to Christianity flows unequivocally from his rebellious instinct; the activities of the missionaries produce such a tranquilizing effect on Nwoye because of his initial disatisfaction with the manly urgings in the traditional set-up. At the same time, the attentive reader is interested in how what is an authentically African or Igbo personality is being negotiated through the contrast drawn between the divergent reactions of Nwoye and his father, a die-hard traditionalist, for whom the doings of the missionaries bring on a grave indignation. By emphasizing the way in which Nwoye's conversion precipitates the rage that subsequently results in Okonkwo's tragic fall, *Things Fall Apart* demonstrates Achebe's ability to work within the conventions of Western tragedy in which the flawed principal character is brought down from lofty heights through the instrumentality of forces unleashed both externally as well as internally. Nevertheless, this presentation deflects critical attention away from the communities that bore the agony of colonization, an enterprise that will ultimately affect everyone in equal measure, while focusing on the lonely hero. It is a falsification of the actual events that occurred during the subjugation of Igboland.

Given the monumental nature of the break-up of the traditional order, Achebe made a terrible mistake with this novel by failing to show sufficient interest in the details of the day-to-day operation of the colonial administration or in how the European conquest became a reality in the first place. What is particularly indefensible is the decision to depict colonization as an essentially benevolent enterprise. This approach gives undue importance to the role of the missionaries and the *osu* caste practice as factors in the defeat of the Igbo by the colonialists. The author suggests that the success of colonization can be traced to the cracks that ostensibly existed in the traditional order. This view holds that the marginalization of certain Igbo groups in the life of their communities—social, moral, political, spiritual, and economic—constituted one of the principal factors that left the segregated people easy prey to what Oladele Taiwo has called "the combined forces of British Administration and Christianity."[31] Although the perceived injustices embedded in the *osu* caste helped the infiltration of the traditional order by foreign invaders, Achebe never makes a clear presentation of what it really means to be an *osu*. In the novel, the outcasts, seeing that the Christianity, which the British used as preparation groundwork for the colonial rule, "welcomed twins and such abomination, thought that it was possible that they would also be received. And so, one Sunday two of them went into the church."[32]

Things Fall Apart indicates that because there were so many marginalized people in traditional society, they were easily co-opted by the missionaries, thus inhibiting the formation of a united opposition movement. If, instead, the narrative had concerned itself more with the essence of the *osu*, with their experience and individual psychology, the novel might be more persuasive in its premise. Instead, the novel makes much, in a generalized manner, of issues concerning the undermining effects that the practices of the *osu* and the killing of twins had on the collective will of the tribe, therefore, the reader hardly knows much about the real experience of the *osu*.

> He was a person dedicated to a god, a thing set apart—a taboo forever, and his children after him. He could neither marry nor be married by a free-born. He was in fact an outcast, living in a special area of the village, close to the Great Shrine. Wherever he went he carried with him the mark of his forbidden caste—long, tangled and dirty hair. A razor was a taboo to him. An *osu* could not attend an assembly of the free born, and they, in turn, could not shelter under his roof. He could not take any of the four titles of the clan, and when he died he was buried by his kind in the evil Forest.[33]

In failing to delineate precisely what it means to be such an outsider, the author does not allow us to see the full force of the discontent erupt that might have motivated these outcasted elements in their rebellious actions. It may well be that this is a point the author himself realized later and attempted to correct with the more elaborate presentation made of the *osu* dilemma through the involved portrait of Clara's suffereing in *No Longer at Ease*.[34]

Moreover, presenting the colonial venture in Umuofia (or Igboland and Africa in general) as a benevolent enterprise seems evasive to the informed reader, who is aware of the deep economic interests that lurk within the colonialist mission. Gareth Griffths has attempted to defend this error by using European interpretive conventions that, by their very nature, privilege the reticence in Achebe's text. Griffths expresses admiration for Achebe's ability to combine cool artistry with a quiet moral vision as well as what he terms the use of the technique of naming without venturing bothersome details. The problem that his approach reveals endorses Achebe's effort to solve the problem of colonization by wishing it away, by not talking about it more fully.

> In his attempt to present a picture of the destruction of tribal Iboland, Achebe is aware that in gaining the voice to speak he reveals his involvement with the destruction which he records. That is why there is no simple condemnation possible, not for Okonkwo, nor Nwoye, nor even for the commissioner. Neither is there any temptation to sentimentalize. The search is not for a lost idyll, nor an historical excuse, but for a meaningful appraisal of what has been lost and what gained, and a clear analysis of where the writer and his contemporaries stand in the list of residual legatees.[35]

This argument not only offers an endorsement of colonization, of the status quo, of the reckless conquest of one people by another, but its recommendation of surface realism as the most valid method for purposes of historical reconstruction reveals a hidden political agenda. There is a fear of looking at the causes that lie behind the surface events. If writers from former colonies dig deeply, it may lead to more explosive literature. A Western liberal may be excused for such an analysis. But when a native writer expresses such attitudes it is simply reactionary.

It is no wonder that, following his unconditional submission to indoctrination by European ideas of progress, which validate colonization, Achebe naively counts the blessings that ostensibly came with the colonial conquest in terms of the schools, hospitals, and the money economy. Readers must ask where his true feelings lie.

> There were many men and women in Umuofia who did not feel as strongly as Okonkwo about the new dispensation. The white man had indeed brought a lunatic religion, but he had also built a trading store and for the first time palm-oil and kernel became things of great price, and much money flowed into Umuofia.
>
> And even in the matter of religion there was a growing feeling that there might be something in it after all, something vaguely akin to method in the overwhelming madness.[33]

This unfortunate passage presses to an irritatingly morbid extreme the worship of the new god; a mindless veneration of money. One wonders why the question is not asked: Money for what? What is the value of money if it does not bring any improvement to the lives of the people? To paraphrase, in what ways did the material trappings that came officially with colonization to Igboland make the people better off than they were before colonization? Because the novel's argument is presented as though money had intrinsic value in itself, it disregards the real price that the people had to pay in spiritual, psychological or emotional, and political terms, and it fatally misses the whole import of what a colonial economy signifies.

Of course, the fact that the Igbos and other Africans had successfully run their economies for ages before colonization (see Boahen, *African Perspectives on Colonialism*, especially Chapter 1), indicates that from the beginning of African history money was always peripheral to life and living. Contrary to what critics like Gareth Griffiths and David Carroll, as well as Achebe himself, would have us believe, what we see is not merely an example of objective historical analysis, but a dangerous equivocation that reveals a tragic unwillingness and/or inability to pierce through the ideological subterfuges of colonialism to display fully and comprehensively its repercussions. In light of information about the author's education and upbringing, it is difficult for one to disregard the silent spaces and absent narratives in *Things Fall Apart* as mere indication of genuine ignorance. More correctly, they point to partisan interests, imperfectly concealed.

One reason the novel's plot opens itself to a skepticism that is at once historical and moral is the misjudgment that attributes a matter as serious as cultural disintegration to an episode involving someone as trifling as the native informant. The use of the death of Okonkwo to signal the end of innocence is inappropriate, not only because using death for the sense of an ending is always suspect, but, more importantly, because the reader finds it difficult to accept that Okonkwo's murder of a puppet is crime sufficiently grave enough to cause the collapse of an entire community especially since, in the past, the murder of a noble kinsman by the same person had been punished merely by banishment.[36]

In concluding this commentary on *Things Fall Apart*, there is an imperative that must be stressed: It is not enough to apply aesthetic considerations to the book. We must evaluate its underlying structure. This novel's treatise is usually considered a model of imaginative historical reconstruction, and it is a common practice to refer to it whenever there is discussion of the way primitive, rural customs were transformed. Its innocent portrayal of social change is often exhalted. There is more at stake in Africa than an arresting story, however. For all its acclaimed aesthetic merits, Achebe's presentation in *Things Fall Apart* rarely goes beyond the surface of events. Carefully examined, one discovers that Achebe uses fictional techniques that one expects from European writers in representing others, not from an African dealing with his society.

Though *Things Fall Apart* is limited by its inability to show the complex interplay of forces during the colonization of Igboland, *Arrow of God*, its sequel, gains its impact largely from the sophisticated way it explores the class collaboration, manipulations, lies, and superior technology of the invaders. It does all this while including a fair amount of the cultural information seen in its predecessor. It is evident in *Arrow of God* (as it is not in *Things Fall Apart*) that Achebe has realized the pitfalls of representing colonization as a quintessentially humanitarian venture. His re-representation of the subject, though informed by the same liberal aesthetic vision, is not only more accurate because it takes into account that a combination of factors led to the colonization of Igboland, it approximates more closely the actual experience of colonization and the Igbo response to it.

Arrow of God is a supremely political novel, and its newest contribution to the project of historical reconstruction lies in unambiquously highlighting how religion and politics were bound together during colonization. What makes *Arrow of God* particularly interesting is its success in integrating the theme of spiritual displacement within a larger political framework. It is as much a story of a community's fall from a state of religious peace into anarchy as it is of the conquest of an oral society by the written word.

The narrative documents the attendant sense of hopelessness with a rare insight, and the concern with politics is not pressed to the disadvantage of formal structure. Where its predecessor inappropriately concentrated on the career of a lonely hero, *Arrow of God* shifts the focus fittingly to Igbo communal experience or history. Charles Nnolim attributes this novelistic achievement primarily to the anthropological text of Simon Alagboga Nnolim, claiming that his *The History of Umuchu* constitutes "the single most important source—in fact, the only source—for *Arrow of God*."[37] His view is not fully supported. Although the importance of indigenous data in the overall design of *Arrow of God* cannot be denied, especially the role of oral tradition in reconstructing the history of colonization of Iboland, the book represents an original and fascinating use of tradition.

Arrow of God was published after *No Longer at Ease*, but it is more directly an extension of the themes in *Things Fall Apart*. In the continuing exploration of a tribal society's response to change, *Arrow of God* not only uses a more extensive body of inside information, it does so with exceptional sensitivity and with greater insight. It updates the experiences of a cluster of pre-colonial Igbo villages that had come together to create the god *Ulu* in order to protect themselves against the slave raiders known as the Abam Warriors. *The* greatest accomplishment of *Arrow of God* is its delineation of how the Abam scourge is displaced by a new enemy: the colonialists who come wearing three different faces, as administrator (or political man), missionary, and soldier. By adroitly integrating the novel's major themes—the land struggle between the two neighboring villages of Okperi and Umuaro, and the leadership struggles of two individuals within the villages who inadvertently assist the foreign invasion by hastening the disintegration of the communities—Achebe reveals his skills as a socio-political documentator. *Arrow of God* presents a detailed record of how the colonizers make use of the conflict between two equally powerful titled elders, Ezeulu and Ezidemili (who is supported by Nwaka, another ambitious individual).

Though the book seems to support once again the theory of disunity as a factor in the conquest of the Igbo community, overall, the plot of *Arrow of God* is not only more unified but more sophisticated in its implementation of narrative techniques that enable the work to reveal the colonial conquest in all of its complex disguises. Documentation in *Arrow of God* is more vivid and more realistic than in *Things Fall Apart.* Two principal reasons that *Arrow of God* is the more successful in its depiction of colonization: First, it presents the encounter as one that encompasses every facet of society. Second, it captures a sense of psychological realism as much as sociological truth. The European takeover involves a displacement of all of the traditional structures of authority, as colonization first questioned, and then replaces local organizational frameworks with alternative ones that create grave disharmony in the lives of Africans. Achebe demonstrates, literally, that the onslaught may appear unspeakable, that describing the repercusions may be nearly impossible, but it is worth a try.

The imposed European structures include the church, which replaced traditional religious rituals; the formal schools (that displaced the conventional moonlight games and hearths as sites to educate children); and the administrative machinery, which now conducted the day-to-day dispensation of justice and rural development (road and bridge building), roles formerly performed by the age-grade groups and secret fraternities.

The more we explore the broad canvas *Arrow of God* uses to enact the drama of colonial invasion, the more we perceive the sheer breadth and multiplicity of the onslaught. In *Arrow of God*, Achebe shows himself to be an adept story-teller. The logical relationship he establishes between the European presence and the collapse of tradition gives eloquent testimony to his skills: first in his handling of the European involvement in the land dispute between the communities of Umuaro and Okperi; and second, in his handling of Ezeulu's lethal confrontation with the conquerors.

The land disputes of Okperi and Umuaro predate the colonial invasion, but many people in Umuaro blame the British presence for the dispute's escalation. Nwaka voices the frustration of these people during a debate: "It is due to the white man who says, like an elder to two fighting children: You will not fight while I am around. And so the younger and weaker of the two begins to swell himself up and to boast."[38] Nwaka accuses the colonialists of being partial to the friendly people of Okperi, since the Okperis have granted the invaders land for settlement by the missionaries (the white district commissioner, Captain Winterbottom, is stationed at the Okperi mission). The garbled version of the story Winterbottom tells Mr. Clarke, the new assistant district officer recently sent out to Africa from England, is evidence of this favoritism.

Examining Winterbottom's story leads us to the second reason for Achebe's superlative success in *Arrow of God*: He places emphasis upon capturing a sense of psychological realism as much as he does on sociological truth. In the story Winterbottom loves to recount regularly, he casts the people of Okperi as peace-loving— as opposed to the supposedly troublesome people of Umuaro. Since Winterbottom makes slight alterations with each telling of the story, he employs stratagems that are reminiscent of the style of the traditional storytellers. Ironically, he looks down on the storytellers, exhibiting an attitude that places him in the grand tradition of the charmed European anthropologist doing field work in Africa, which, in a sense, is what he is. Thus, it is not surprising that we learn far more from his story about the psychology of the colonizer than any direct descriptions could provide:

> This war between Umuaro and Okperi began in a rather interesting way.... a man from Umuaro went to visit a friend in Okperi one fine morning and after he'd had one or two gallons of palmwine—it's quite incredible how much of that dreadful stuff they can tuck away—anyhow, this man from Umuaro having drunk his friend's palmwine reached for his ikenga and split it into two...[39]

Amid all of the fairytales and willful distortions, this is a chilling picture of British condescension towards the Igbos. By deriding what the ikenga means, "the most important fetish in the Ibo [sic] man's arsenal [which] represents his ancestors to whom he must make daily sacrifice," Winterbottom makes a comedy out of a very grave situation that has involved the loss of human life. By reducing the complex conflict into a simple story about primitive customs, Winterbottom robs it of its true weight. The premise upon which he bases his actions is particularly risky, because it is a mixture of half-truths and lies. Winterbottom's observation that when a man dies among the Igbo his *ikenga* must be "split into two; and half is buried with him and the other half is thrown away" may be basically sound, the deductions he makes from it are totally reductive: "[Y]ou can see the implication of what our friend from Umuaro did in splitting his host's fetish. This was, of course, the greatest sacrilege. The outraged host reached for his gun and blew the other fellow's head off. And so a regular war developed between the two villages, until I stepped in."[40] Winterbottom's version is entirely insensitive to the cursing, the threatening personal assault, which provokes the retaliatory act.

In his book *Chinua Achebe*, David Carroll views the relationship between Africans and Europeans as one dogged by a grave "mutual misunderstanding" (99). While such a position might free the critic from any obligation to probe Winterbottom's motives—that he acts not from ignorance but viciousness, that he pretends to know what he does not really know for selfish reasons—it smacks of special pleading. His persistent belief that Winterbottom "knows his Africans well" and is someone whose judgment ought to be trusted because he is not simply "an embittered 'Old Coaster'" is simultaneously true and misleading, because it is a posture that carefully occludes any attempt to tease out the cultural assumptions compelling Winterbottom to undertake actions intended to deform the African.[41] According to Carroll, however, in the same passage,

> [H]e [Winterbottom] knows the country well, understands the Igbo language, and acts according to the values he believes in. And parody works in the opposite direction too. The villagers assume similarly defensive and exaggerated postures later in the novel when they seek to contain

the encroachments of Europeans. So long as the two worlds of the novel remain unintelligible to each other they act in a similar way in face of the unknown. The Europeans seek refuge behind their myths and rituals as they strive to administer this corner of empire. They are looking for a power structure they can understand and promote: if they cannot find one, they will have to create it.

What Carroll ignores is that it is precisely the wholesale transfer of European logic to the local situation—as if the Igbo were the same as Europeans—that prevents Winterbottom from getting to know the Igbos well. The Africans may be overwhelmingly perplexed by the actions of the foreigners, but the assumption that the stranger can in any way know the situation of the indigeneous people better than they themselves can ever hope to is wrong-headed in the extreme. On the contrary, imperialist interests defied native logic. The native people's resentment of the British draws its animus from the duplicity of the invader who understood so well the yearning of the natives to maintain their freedom but found it in the way of the irrepressible economic and political interests of an expanding imperialism. The familiar posture of the colonial administrator, standing aloof on government hill, examining the actions of the natives with total detachment and often disparaging them but claiming to understand their real motivations better than the "actors" themselves, is emblematic of unlimited colonial arrogance.

If Winterbottom, the mighty representative of imperialism, does not show the slightest interest in, or the ability to understand, native logic, it is not because of any personal inadequacies. Rather, as the man charged with furthering the expansion of Empire, Winterbottom has no real choice: the dream of an expanding Empire is what he must defend. Central to Winterbottom's goals, and crucial to the interests of the imperial power, is the maintenance of peace and order within native domains—not protection of the interests of the natives as such. That is the reason Winterbottom disarms the two warring parties by confiscating their guns, but without making any serious effort to get to the root of the conflict—the land question.

Winterbottom's bearing belies all of the claims of colonization's "civilizing mission"—the idea that the British were discharging the burden of carrying civilization to Africans. Far from merely expressing individual nastiness, however, Winterbottom's actions simply manifest corporate greed, selfishness, and ethnocentric intolerance run amuck. In opposition to the Euro-centric view-point expressed by Winterbottom, that the Igbos were tearing each other apart for very frivolous reasons before the onset of British "humanitarian mission," this novel presents the true picture: The people had been at relative peace with themselves and their neighbors; although occasional conflicts did arise, there were channels for resolving them amicably. Thus Achebe disproves the idea of the African's innate barbarity and places on record the great land pressures that made land a precious commodity, for the possession of which communities had to struggle, a struggle that the colonizer not only fuels but capitalizes upon to establish their hegemonic control.

Arrow of God succeeds so thoroughly in its objective not only to demonstrate that before colonization, the Igbos were a highly intelligent group that had full control of both their circumstances and their environment, but also in its obvious objective to acknowledge the openness to opposing ideas, the basis of Igbo democracy, an attribute that unwittingly assisted in rendering the community vulnerable to the Western onslaught. That not even a figure as powerful as Ezeulu can enforce his will upon his community (he is unable to stop its war drive or even to decide the destiny of his own children), may be evidence of the Igbo republican outlook, but it is this attitude that eventually proves the bane of the society.

A disastrous consequence of the extreme competitiveness that the Igbo federation encourages is the fierceness with which individuals like Nwaka and Ezeulu press their egotistic claims, to the point where such pursuits become inimical to the sense of communal oneness. Thus, once Ezeulu begins to dissuade Umuaro from warring with Okperi over the disputed piece of land, because his father told him the land belonged to Okperi, his argument gives his arch-rival, Nwaka, the opportunity to counter with an even more persuasive argument by stating that his own father told him a different story. The charges of nepotistic tendencies that Nwaka levels at Ezeulu are especially inflammatory.

These acrimonious debates, which lowered communal morale and the necessary cohesiveness to resist colonization effectively, prove calamitous. The community's internal strife leaves the invaders free to help themselves to as much of the land as they desire.

Nwaka and Ezeulu are two self-confident individuals who have mastered the art of public-speaking, but they fail to realize that it is only by coming together they can effectively resist their greatest enemy—the external invader—who seeks control not just over their land but also over their bodies and spirit as well. The fact that both use their gifts for their society's destruction is lamentable because the linguistic devices they employ, as Emmanuel Ngara points out, can be used not only to foster cultural unity within the tribe but also to rally political support against the foreign occupation of their territory.[42]

In the traditional Igbo society, oratory was an asset that required proper skill. In numerous exchanges, Nwaka and Ezeulu do not recognize the import of discretionary speech. Here is an example of one of Nwaka's stimulating performances:

> '... Elders and Ndiche of Umuaro, let everyone return to his house if we have no heart in the fight. We shall not be the first people who abandoned their farmland or even their homestead to avoid war. But let us not tell ourselves or our children that we did it because the land belonged to other people. Let us rather tell them that their fathers did not choose to fight. Let us tell them also that we marry the daughters of Okperi and their men marry our daughters, and that where there is this mingling men lose the heart to fight. Umofia kwenu!' (16)

By appealing to the elemental democratic spirit of the Igbo, Nwaka's speech is persuasive in seeming to abandon coercion and force. In this part of his speech, Nwaka turns all the pro-peace arguments on their heads; his appeals to the traditional sense of Igbo gallantry show that he has thoroughly internalized the value system of his community. Because Nwaka's speech can be interpreted as ultimately a rallying cry to action, it is not an exaggeration to say that the blow-out that follows the Umuaro delegation to Okperi has been foreshadowed, provoked by the sentiments in Nwaka's speech.

Even before starting out, the mission of the Akukalia-led team was already a done deal: If the group inflexibly presses its community's ownership claims, it is because its mandate requires it to do so. Every listener knows Umuaro has decided to go to war to reclaim the disputed land; the so-called peace mission is merely a tradition-bound formality. This is why the team regards Ogbuefi Egonwanne's warning as merely a manner of speaking. The old man advised: "'We do not want Okperi to choose war; nobody eats war. If they choose peace we shall rejoice. But whatever they say you are not to dispute with them. Your duty is to bring word back to us."' (17).

Because choosing peace would have entailed Okperi's renouncing its claims to the land, war was inevitable. Ezeulu is correct in describing the Akukalia-led mission as a contradiction in terms: "[O]ne of the oldest men in Umuaro . . . wants to teach our emissary how to carry fire and water in the same mouth."[43] Ezeulu equates such an assignment with the mission of "a boy sent by his father to steal [who] does not go stealthily but breaks the door with his feet."[44] Akukalia shows the exuberance expected of him by engaging in a heated argument that provokes his host to use an inflammatory word. This forces the visitor to commit the sacrilege of rushing to his host's family shrine and breaking his *ikenga*, "the strength of his right arm."[45] Stunned by what the host considers an unprovoked attack on his ancestors, the man Ebo kills his attacker and the two communities are drawn into a bitter war, one from which the British emerge victorious.

Arrow of God is a major fictional exploration of the psychology of power—how to obtain it, what it means to wield it, and the consequences of any attempt to monopolize authority. If Ezeulu and Nwaka exemplify the destructive effects that inevitably accompany the quest to obtain exclusive control, Ezeulu's son Edogo can be viewed as the embodiment of the frustration that ultimately comes with an unsuccessful power struggle. Achebe shows that the agony that arises from a frustrated power quest, that a sense of powerlessness can be no less unsettling than the self-inflated conceit that comes with the excessive exercise of power.

Edogo dramatically articulates ideas about the destructive capacity of power, for through his relationship with his father, the generational conflict of values seeking to shape social institutions is emphasized. The opposition is between a refined artistic sensibility, Edogo, and an unyielding religious one, Ezeulu; both vying for absolute political authority. Ezeulu's personal qualities assist in the destruction of both the unbending protagonist and the conservative tradition he represents. The peaceful picture of Ezeulu's family in the novel's opening pages, with children playing happily in the moonlit night, is suddenly undercut when we see the reality of the adult world in Ezeulu's family torn apart by competition, bickering, and animosity. At the center of this discord is Ezeulu, a father who should be the symbol of unity and love, but whose suppression of dialogue has caused a communication breakdown within his household:

> The trouble with Ezeulu was that he could never see something and take his eyes away from it .... That was what their father could never learn. He must go on treating his grown children like little boys, and if they ever said no there was a big quarrel. This was why the older his children grew the more he seemed to dislike them. (91)

Edogo's conflict with his father brings to the surface Ezeulu's ambivalence, mental instability, and inscrutability. Bitterness and hate dominate Edogo's thinking whenever he "remembered what his mother used to say when she was alive... that Ezeulu's only fault was that he expected everyone — his wives, his kinsmen, his children, his friends and even his enemies — to think and act like himself. Anyone who dared to say no to him was an enemy."[46]

Ultimately, the novel gathers support for Edogo in his belief that Ezeulu's attempt to deny the family members the opportunity to realize their full potential as individuals, his unwillingness to grant full autonomy to his children, arises from Ezeulu's acute self-centeredness. There is good reason for Edogo to be convinced that his father had sent Oduche to join the white man's religion as a ploy "to disqualify him for the priesthood of Ulu."[47] The soft spot Ezeulu has for Nwafo, his youngest son, gives further credence to his partiality. In an attempt to gain relief from the tense atmosphere at home, Edogo spends prolonged periods carving wood in the secluded spirit house. Ezeulu's determination to deprive his oldest son of freedom is proof of Ezeulu's domineering insistence that nothing would stop him from attempting to stifle the creative intellect itself, the moving force of his son's life. However, the fact that the artistic vocation does little to assuage Edogo's political ambition may be the book's way of saying that creative and political needs are not always met by equal or identical means.

It is difficult to understand why the novel does not explore in greater depth the theme of the difference between the artistic and political cravings. On the contrary, the thematic focus is on the giddiness produced by the exercise of exclusive authority and the impossibility of anyone holding such power surrendering it voluntarily. Though it may seem logical that whoever wants power must seize it for himself, the wisdom is lost on Edogo, whose unfulfilled political ambition is to have power handed over to him on a golden platter. This evokes the magnitude of distress that accompanies being bereft of any form of political authority. When Edogo goes to unburden himself to his father's closest friend Akuebue, it is in a bid to enlist the elderly man's help in resolving the one problem uppermost in Edogo's mind. Little does he know that he will achieve the opposite of his desires.

Edogo's visit to Akuebe is an act of desperation. He is propelled by an awareness of his father's plot to deny him his legitimate inheritance, the succession to the *Ulu* priesthood. Not only does his political passivity incite unwanted ridicule, Edogo's inarticulateness is a legitimate ground for the disdained treatment towards him. The more Edogo strains for effect by searching for the ultimate means of expression, e.g., resorting to the use of riddles, the more he alienates himself from the man whose heart and ear he wants so desperately to win:

> Edogo told him that the reason why Ezeulu sent Oduche to the new religion was to leave the way clear for Nwafo to become Chief Priest.
>
> 'Who said so?' asked Akuebue. But before Edogo could answer he added: 'You speak about Nwafo and Oduche, what about you and Obika?'
>
> 'Obika's mind is not on such things — neither is mine.'
>
> 'But Ulu does not ask if a man's mind is on something or not. If he wants you he will get you. Even the one who has gone to the new religion, if Ulu wants him he will take him.'
>
> 'That is true,' said Edogo. 'But what worries me is that my father makes Nwafo think he will be chosen. If tomorrow as you say Ulu chooses another person there will be strife in

the family. My father will not be there then and it will all rattle around my own head'. (126)

Thematically and stylistically, this is a key episode in the novel. It not only dramatizes the dangerous domestic squabbles that Ezeulu's mishandling of the succession to the *Ulu* chieftaincy has unleashed, but also brings starkly to the surface the rancor and bitterness created by the politics of exclusion that the chief priest of *Ulu* is playing. Although succession ought ideally to be a spiritual appointment, Ezeulu is handling it as though it were purely a political one. Edogo has a stake in this matter, but he is annoyingly intent upon suppressing his true feelings. Akuebe feels "pity and a little contempt" for Edogo: Pity because Akuebe can understand the pain of being arbitrarily passed over; contempt because Akuebe believes that a man who wants something badly should have the courage to "open his mouth like a man and say that he wanted" it.[48] Edogo's hiding "behind Oduche and Obika," reveals to Akuebe nothing but a lethal combination of cowardice and dishonesty. In the end, Akuebe is not the solution Edogo had expected.

Critics have made much of the imprisonment that prevents Ezeulu from eating the three ritual yams as an issue in the disintegration of the tribal society, but have so far sidelined the contribution made by Obika's death. Until we view Obika's death logically—as an intervention by the gods on behalf of the unjustly treated Edogo—it is impossible to see its central position within the overall structure of the crises explored in the novel. To be sure, Ezeulu's prison ordeal exerts enormous influence on all his subsequent actions. Ezeulu's power problems are exacerbated by the summons he receives from the administrator at Okperi. To show that his overriding loyalty is to his community, Ezeulu calls an assembly of the elders to inform them of the summons. When he fails to obtain the expected support and encouragement, Ezeulu is disappointed, even embittered. The obvious source of Ezeulu's frustration is his awareness that the community could not contain the malice of his arch-enemy, Nwaka, who accuses Ezeulu of attempting to secretly cultivate friendship with the white enemy while cleverly turning to his kinsmen to lend legitimacy to his actions. The retaliatory grudges that Ezeulu has begun to nurse against the clan lead to his suicidal refusal to perform the ritual function of eating all the required sacred yams in order to cleanse society. Although this omission is the proximate cause that forces the members of his community to turn to the white man's god for protection, a remote cause for the collapse of the old order is Edogo's untimely death.

We should not pass quickly over the role Obika's death plays in the whole scenario, because all of the mishap that visits the Chief Priest can subsequently be traced to his initial mishandling of the *Ulu* chieftaincy. Ezeulu's attempt to choose his own successor, contrary to tradition, and the meddling interest he takes in the rivalry of his children, convince Edogo that his father sent Oduche to join the white man's religion to "disqualify him for the priesthood of Ulu."[49] Despite the unwavering opposition of family members, Ezeulu remains adamant in his decision to send Oduche to school. Oduche's sacrilegeous act of attempting to kill a royal python confirms the rightness of the clan's position. The attack from Nwaka, as well as from clan members, initiated by Ezeulu's testimony against his clan in the land case, draws much of its strength from the Chief Priest's acts of apostasy. The pattern of misdemeanor, forcefully brought out in Ezeulu's attempt to pass over Edogo for the chieftaincy, makes it clear that fate could not remain indifferent to the community's feelings. That the experienced district commissioner, Captain Winterbottom, is hospitalized—leaving Ezeulu's case to the inexperienced Mr. Clarke—is an expression of the gods' active interest in human affairs.

The role of spirituality, the idea of the gods engaging in a crusade for retributive justice, is missing in Oladele Taiwo's discussion of this episode in *Culture and the Nigerian Novel*, which presents it as an illustration of the dehumanization of the Igbos by the colonial administration. For me, the event also shows the novel's masterly integration of spiritual and secular concerns. In Taiwo's words, Ezeulu's sentencing demonstrates that "the feeling of superiority on the part of British political officers often stands in the way of the effective implementation of the Indirect Rule system and makes direct contact with the people impossible."[50] The way Clarke and his subordinates misinterpret Ezeulu's resolute position is a clear instance of colonial insolence. The officers whom Clarke delegates to handle Ezeulu's case refuse to listen to Ezeulu, whose crime is that he is simply too proud to cooperate with them. Having ruled out dialogue, the colonial administration has no way of considering the precarious situation of the Chief Priest: Tradition does not permit Ezeulu to be anybody's chief except *Ulu*'s.

While all of the power plays, intrigues, disappointments, and insecurities that cause chaos in the lives of the officers are shown to contribute to a misinterpretation of Ezeulu's motives, the officers' overdetermination ultimately suggests the possibility of the gods' deep involvement in the matter. In light of the clear intersection between religion and politics, Wole Soyinka is misleading when he alleges that the work gives him "a genuine feeling of being cheated" through its "dogged secularization of the profoundly mystical."[51] Because the complex interplay of forces makes clear distinctions between religious and political motivations impossible, by paying scrupulous attention to the details of events that follow Ezeulu's imprisonment, in *Arrow of God*, Achebe shows himself a conscientious storyteller.

If *Arrow of God* gives as close a view as a novel can capture of the total chemistry of colonialism, it is not only because it proves the duplicity of colonialism's claims to order, but also because it reveals with resounding success the Igbos as playthings in the hands of their gods. In about the same way, the British officers who punish Africans on the flimsiest of excuses are shown as victims of an ambitiously vicious and manipulative imperialist machine that is beyond their own power to control.[52] *Arrow of God* could capture Ezeulu's inner turmoil by using the same narrative device—the stream of consciousness technique—employed in depicting the world of the colonial officers, because the actions of protagonist and antagonist spring from minds of an identical nature. Both are obsessed with power and are not only fencing but clinging desperately to omnipotence because their desire is for security. All believe that only absolute power to control the actions of others can allay such anxieties. The text's ability to penetrate the minds of both oppressor and oppressed, the psychology of both conqueror and conquered people, is thus intimidatingly stirring.

It is to demonstrate both the largeness of Ezeulu's ego as well as the folly of the attempts of one people to dominate another that the text emphasizes the mark of seething humiliation that Ezeulu's sentencing and jailing causes. The Chief Priest is incensed particularly because his traditional sources of power had been near infinite. The dissolution of those powers is an event without precedence, an ordeal of political disempowerment for which nothing within the imaginable frame of local experience could have prepared Ezeulu. His obstinate resolve to punish the community, surprising as it may seem, is based on awareness that if the foreign tormentors are not within the range of vengeance, Ezeulu's own people are. He thus yields to anger and defeat, as if emotion would reverse the situation, when it would be wiser to listen to the *Ulu*'s warning that the Chief Priest not take vengeance into his own hands. The quick plunge taken by Ezeulu's consciousness, though it demonstrates the intolerability of the state of powerlessness, is the cost for holding too firmly to a crumbling center of power.

Ezeulu degenerates quickly, moving from absolute self-confidence— once boasting that he had graduated from the stage of "dancing to receive presents" and that no one could "know the Thing which beats the drum to which Ezeulu dances"—to mental and psychological disarray.[53] Ezeulu's case is reminiscent of the classic fable about the inflated hero suddenly deflated, the man on the heights who is precipitiously brought down. His fate dramatically defines the pain that pervades the soul forced to endure the predicament of political rejection. Given the inclemency of Ezeulu's rejection by the community that elected him to leadership, his ending is predictable: His boundless bitterness can only lead to self-destruction and more. To follow the graph of Ezeulu's disequilibrium is to follow the text's concern with the mental theater of its protagonist's mind.

Obiechina has summarized the change in these events beautifully, and his review deserves detailed attention. Because of the overwhelming pressure both from within himself and the external world, Ezeulu has abandoned "the effort to mobilize support within his clan" as he instead "sallies out to face his fate single-handed." Having isolated himself when he needed "collective solidarity" the most, Ezeulu is "totally embittered" and is in "an uncompromising mood which is made no better by his being detained for not answering" the administrator's summons promptly. Obiechina continues:

> The rest is a quick plunge into the molten centre of disaster. His two month's detention upset the agricultural calendar because he could not eat his ritual yams while in detention. He refuses to call the Feast of the New Yam until he has

eaten all the remaining yams. The delay in harvesting the yams begins to hurt the people and threaten famine. Desperate and confounded, the people turn to the Christian religion for savaltion. They send their sons with yam offerings to the Christian harvest festival and thereafter harvest their crops in the name of these sons. A tailpiece to the drama is provided by the sudden death of Obika, Ezeulu's favourite son. The Chief Priest goes mad and the people draw their own moral from his tragedy.[54]

Aside from the oversight in the reference to Obika's death as "tailpiece" to the main "drama," Obiechina's is as concise a summary as one can obtain of the events. The oversight is significant, however, since Obika's death is a central issue. Obika's demise sounds the death knell of tradition in this novel; Ezeulu's dirge captures the depth of his overpowering grief, which so incapacitates the father he is unable to resist the European assault.

Indeed, Ezeulu particularly finds great cause for grief in the death of Obika, because of its poor timing. The circumstances surrounding Obika's death make it an event that robs Ezeulu's life, and all life, of meaning.

Ezeulu sank to the ground in utter amazement. It was not simply the blow of Obika's death, great though it was. Men had taken greater blows: that was what made a man a man. For did they not say that a man is like a funeral lamb which must take whatever beating comes to it without opening its mouth; that the silent tremor of pain down its body alone must tell of its suffering?

At any other time Ezeulu would have been more than a match to his grief. He would have been equal to any pain not compounded with humiliation. But why, he asked himself again and again, why had Ulu chosen to deal thus with him, to strike him down and then cover him with mud? What was his offence? Had he not divined the god's will and obeyed it? When was it ever heard that a child was scalded by the piece of yam its own mother put in its palm? What man would send his son with potsherd to bring fire from a neighbour's hut and then unleash rain on him? Who ever sent his son up the palm to gather nuts and then took an axe and felled the tree? But today such a thing had happened before the eyes of all. What could it point to but the collapse and the ruin of all things?[55]

Ezeulu's grief is colored by his correct interpretation of Obika's death as an unwarrantable act of betrayal vented by the very gods he depends upon; this is why he says the breach of faith parallels a child's tragic deception by its father. Support for such a position is provided by the reliable narrator, who equates Ezeulu's predicament to that of "a man who, unlike lesser men, always goes to battle without a shield because he knows that bullets and matchet strokes will glance off his medicine-boiled skin" but, who, discovers in "the thick of the battle that the power has suddenly, without warning, deserted him."[56]

Arrow of God doesn't make any great claims of visionary projection, restricted as its concerns are to historical and socio-political analysis. In it, Achebe achieves a greater level of success than he does with *Things Fall Apart*; i.e., portraying the traumatic moment when Africa and Europe were brought together in that ghastly collision now known as colonization. *Arrow of God* is an intensely coherent novel, one with a narrative tension that matches the intensity of the conflicts it investigates. Read it with care; it provides no foundation for G. D Killam's allegation that he finds "much in the novel which has little direct relation to the story the novel has to tell."[57] Though short on prescription, *Arrow of God* more than makes up for it by the details it provides of the interplay of forces responsible for the defeat of the Igbo by the British. Its greatest achievement is the balance it establishes between the compulsion to draw Africans up essentially as victims of colonization on the one hand and the recognition, on the other hand, that individuals may also have a hand in shaping their own destiny. With such a balance secured, it is no wonder that the attempt to present a record of the choas left behind by colonization is so convincingly executed.

Chapter 3

THE INDIGENOUS LEADERSHIP IN PRE- AND POST-INDEPENDENCE BLACK AFRICA

(BLACK ELITES, EDUCATORS, POLITICIANS, BUSINESSMEN AND WOMEN, AND THE MILITARY DICTATORS)

The idea of colonial rule may induce the picture of an army of foreign soldiers, police personnel, priests, educators, and administrative officers—all dressed in full gear and patrolling all of the nooks and corners of occupied territories. In truth, however, native peoples only occasionally saw a white face during the period of British colonial rule in Africa. In Igboland, in particular, large tracts of land were poorly policed—even by native personnel. There, colonial rule was largely indirect: The colonialists mostly used a crop of local lackeys to rule and exploit the hinterland. White colonial officers did not need to soil their own hands, so to speak, because a handful of powerful local allies was all they needed to get the job done efficiently. Formal education, the key means by which Africans were prepared for colonial service, therefore served not only as a vehicle of neutralizing instruction but as a means of access to elite roles.

This chapter discusses *No Longer at Ease*, *A Man of the People*, and *Anthills of the Savannah*, as works exploring the impact of Western education. In these, Achebe courses through the history of Western education in Nigeria, beginning with the colonial context (when its effects on the educated Africans were mainly psychological) and moving to the post-independence era (when its backlash on administration begins to be felt deeply).

A great deal of energy has been put into debating the cultural and educational background, which Achebe is believed to have drawn upon in composing his books, but the close relationship between his personal experiences and that of his fictional doubles has so far eluded critical attention.[1] Although *No Longer at Ease*, for example, stands on its own as compelling fictional narrative, knowing that it is a creative validation of the author's own experiences enriches our grasp of how autobiographical fiction—the most intimate and revealing of literary genres—offers an expansive vision of a community's collective memory. Restating literature's ability to draw animation from a writer's lived experience, John Hollander, an indefatigable poet and literary critic, remarks about the raw courage needed to open up the self candidly. Whereas some writers muster the guts to lay open their hearts, others are too reserved to do:

> Poets will always want privately to flee the spider's web woven of affiliations spun by others—sociologically minded others, in particular, with no aesthetic and moral agendas. Frequently, this flight will take them into intended or unwitting evasion, idiosyncratically brandished like a standard, sanctuary taken in a position that being acknowledged as making—to invoke W. H. Auden's triad—redeems one from impure necessities of knowing or judging.[2]

In *No Longer at Ease*, Achebe crafts a work of such rare courage. Achebe uses the educational experiences of the book's protagonist, Obi Okonkwo (his fictional double) to represent that of others of his generation. In this book, readers are encouraged to view events, people, and places as having direct counterparts in an actual world. Achebe handles the connections so well, one senses the identical past he shares with Obi Okonkwo—beginning with the canonic works (all written by English authors) that both of them were fed at the university: Shakespeare, Milton, and Wordsworth as well as Conrad, Joyce Cary, and Graham Greene.[3]

The unique elements of schooling within British and French imperial systems had previously been assumed; but thanks to a work like *No Longer at Ease*, we now know that the notion that discrepancies exist between education in the metropole and in the colony is wrong in its entirety. According to Madeleine Coltenet-Hage and Kevin Meehan in a recent essay, the idea that the French and English instructional practices were geared toward (and produced) different results is equally wrong. In all cases, as both Achebe in his novel and the pair of Coltenet-Hage and Meehan in their essay show, assimilation is the end view of colonial education. As Coltenet-Hage and Meehan argue, "Given the extent to which all 'civilizing' projects necessarily depend on an educational apparatus, the focus on schooling serves to highlight the *problems* of a colonial formation in microscopic fashion. Colonial schools constitute points of uneasy contact where knowledge, codes, and values coming from *somewhere else* are transmitted, deliberately and forcibly, to a diverse local population."[4]

Coltenet-Hage and Meehan do not mention Achebe's novel in their essay, but their observations are relevant to *No Longer At Ease*, especially in light of their remark about the way colonial education magnifies for those in the colony the existing dysfunctions of the metropole. In British as in Francophone Africa, school is the place where young colonized subjects face the difficult challenge of integrating Western knowledge and values with indigenous knowledge.

No Longer at Ease demonstrates clearly that it is not so much the specific details about the operation of Western schools that should be of paramount importance; rather, it is the inevitable repercussions such foreign instruction ultimately has on Africans. The narrative of *No Longer at Ease* derives its peculiar power from its in-depth exploration of the draw back of such a hostile educational system. Through Obi Okonkwo, an unsuspecting individual, who is a product of that education, Achebe graphically illustrates the mental anguish that an unsuitable educational system causes its African victims. It also maps an insensitive admninistration's exploitation of the indigeneous people, their level of confusion, and ultimate drift from their own cultural center. Readers gain an in-depth appraisal of the performance of the educated Africans as a professional group. Obi is designed as both an individual flesh and blood human and a representative figure.

When Obi's community sends him off to a British university, he could not immediately imagine what weight is attached to his being a major part of a mission for a general socio-political and economic uplift. However, a prayer by one member of his village reveals that Obi's education is conceived of as the community's pragmatic response to change, rather than an end in itself:

> In times past... Umofia would have required of you to fight in her wars and bring home human heads. But these were days of darkness from which we have been delivered by the blood of the lamb of God. Today we send you to bring knowledge. Remember that the fear of the Lord is the beginning of wisdom.[5]

The members of the Lagos branch of the Umofia Progressive Union are even more explicit in their demands. Obi is, they tell him, expected "to read law so that when he returned he would handle all their land cases against their neighbours."[6] The people view Obi as a prized possession. A person of "great honour," Obi is expected to help "the ancient town of Umofia...join the comity of other towns in their match towards political irredentism, social equality and economic emancipation."[7] In other words, the group is counting on Obi to serve as a vital organ of community involvement. The plan is for Obi to help his kinsfolk achieve the much desired parity with the other tribes in the country.

These clan members cannot anticipate Obi's alienation because of their limited information about Western education. However, it has been confirmed that

> the process of education is more complex than that. Not only has it raised his status, it has done something more radical to the whole structure of his personality, something which he cannot reverse even if he would; it has made him see himself as an individual. The dual worlds are not simply those of the village and the rich elite, or of the educated and the uneducated; Obi has also to commute between the corporate world of an integrated society and the lonely world of the individual consciousness.[8]

No Longer at Ease focuses on Obi's moral decline without probing its underlying roots. Obi is represented as morally deficient. The text should clearly present his predicament in the context of the disquieting consequences of the clash between African attitudes and European views and life styles since Obi is evidently one of those unable to reconcile the opposing systems. Indeed, Obi's mental and psychological dislocation indicates how sharp the fundamental cultural divide is.

Obi is particularly suitable for bringinging these conflicts to the surface because he is a transitional figure—the product of both European individualistic tradition and traditional African communalism. Growing up at a time when colonialism had destroyed the indigenous basis of most Africans' economic viability (by restricting access to well-paid jobs to the minority elite of Western educated Africans) gives Obi's first-hand experience of the dilemma unusual credibility. These elite face an unusal quandary. Though obligated to ameliorate the condition of others in their community, they invariably discover, to their chagrin, that they are severely constrained by the limited resources available to them. This predicament is most apparent when Obi finally returns after a prolonged absence from his village. There he discovers the barbarous deterioration in his parents's standard of living:

> Obi did not sleep for a long time after he had lain down. He thought about his responsibilities. It was clear that his parents could no longer stand on their own. They had never relied on his father's meagre pension. He planted yams and his wife planted cassava and coco yams. She also made soap from leachings of palm ash and oil and sold it to the villagers for a little profit. But now they were too old for these things.
>
> 'I must give them a monthly allowance from my salary.' How much? Could he afford ten pounds? If only he did not have to pay twenty pounds a month to the Umofia Progressive Union. Then there was John's school fees. (55)

It was frustrating to know that in his parents' blighted circumstances he was helpless. Based primarily on indices of social advancement or in terms of material success, Obi's parents can be said to have failed by all Igbo standards, because the Igbos place primacy on material well-being, subsequently view old age as the time when people take stock of their life achievements rather than struggle for survival.

Therefore, for all who understand the political economy of imperialism, the poverty of Obi's parents clearly exposes the insensitivity of the system inherited from colonialism. This is a system that espouses a deliberate policy designed to dispossess the poor through its disturbing failure to provide any means of social security for people in times of need. The stunning scene of the dip in fortunes of Obi's parents pointedly mirrors the brutality with which colonialism operates. By displacing traditional mechanisms that had cushioned the underprivileged people from excessive hardship, without replacing those devices with viable alternatives, colonization leaves the subject peoples out in the cold. And, because the salary and perks attached to European posts, such as those of Obi and Clara, were meant to support only the earner and his/her nuclear family, the arrangement leaves someone who bears the burden of extra responsibilities attached to the African extended family with no other option but to look outside of his legitimate source of income for the means of meeting those obligations. Ironically, Obi fails to make such a connection.

Philip Rogers says that Obi could not refuse a bribe because he lacks authentic values. I believe, however, it is because of the material poverty of Obi's own circumstances—not because of any inherent spiritual depravities. According to Rogers,

> Obi's finally accepting a bribe is not the result of a circumstantial trap. Achebe's plot denies Obi such a justification. He accepts the bribe only because he can find no reason to refuse it. Achebe represents Obi's need for money at this time quite vaguely in order to show that it is as much the emptiness of Obi's heart as his pocket that leads to his fall.[9]

Perhaps this manner of disagreement is simultaneously correct and misleading, because it accurately maps the architecture of the plunge that Obi's mind has taken but fails to pinpoint its cause.

The narrative creates the impression that the system of rewards inherent in the unimaginative postcolonial administrative set-up is unsuitable for the African context. Nowhere is there a connection between Obi's corruption and the snares embedded in the system within which he functions. Even Obi himself discovers this belatedly. Having initially dismissed as ridiculous the thought that he sought a civil service post for the sole purpose of enriching himself with bribes, he puts up considerable effort to resist corruption. It is decidedly late when Obi discovers the inescapability of fraud within the neocolonial set-up.

Obi's first glimpse of the problem occurs one day while he is travelling home by public transportation. He has had a job interview and is awaiting the outcome. On the road, he witnesses the spectacle of a lorry suddenly being stopped by a policeman. When the lorry driver tries to extricate himself from trouble with a bribe, Obi's incriminating gaze momentarily scares the policeman, who later regains his composure, and, in an excessive outburst of anger and frustration, promptly issues unspecified charges against the driver and then detains the lorry. When, instead of offering Obi their support, the other passengers join the driver in accusing him of embroiling them in troubles, Obi laments:

> 'What an Augean stable!'.. 'Where does one begin? With the masses? Educate the masses?' He shook his head. 'Not a chance there. It would take centuries. A handful of men at the top. Or even one man with a vision—an enlightened dictator. People are scared of the word nowadays. But what kind of democracy can exist side by side with so much corruption and ignorance? Perhaps a half-way house—a sort of compromise.' (40)

Despite Obi's sneering condescension toward the natives, however, he himself is soon reduced to their level. The process of Obi's perversion is instructive, for it exposes the intractability endemic in the structure of rewards promoted in the civil service. There is abundant evidence in the text to inculpate the impossibility of avoiding corruption.

Most surprising is that Obi falls when he takes success for granted. Despite the efforts of Elsie Mark, a scholarship applicant, and her brother to compromise his integrity, Obi wards them off. However, the gains in moral stature quickly dissipate with the onset of Obi's financial difficulties: Compounded by the repayment of a loan to the Lagos Branch of the Umofia Progressive union due at the same time that his insurance and over-draft fees fall due, Obi must bear the costs of car maintenance, sundry gifts for his clans men, and his electricitry bills as well. Obi's budding will is eroded when he takes his leave allowance, which facilitates his visit to the village. Added to his parents' stiff resistance to his proposal to marry Clara, an *osu*, is another problem:

> Obi had not realized that the allowance was not a free gift to be spent as one liked. He now learnt to his horror that, subject to a maximum of twenty-five pounds, he was allowed to claim so much for every mile of the return journey. Mr Omo called it claiming 'on an actuality basis'.[10]

That "little arithmetic" signals Obi's significant moral decline. Using the mileage chart, Obi lies, telling Mr. Omo that he spent his leave in the Cameroons because "the journey from Lagos to Umofia amounted to only fifteen pounds." This is a significant step in Obi's plunge into corruption. Falsifying leave documents might not seem like a big crime, but, given the idealistic cast of Obi's mind, this action leaves a damaging effect to his moral authority:

> The chief result of the crisis in Obi's life was that it made him examine critically for the first time the mainspring of his actions. And in doing so he uncovered a good deal that he could only regard as sheer humbug. Take this matter of twenty pounds every month to his town union, which in the final analysis was the root cause of all his troubles. Why had he not swallowed his pride and accepted the four month's grace? Could a person in his position afford that kind of pride? Was it not a common saying among his people that a man should not, out of pride and etiquette, swallow his phlegmn?[11]

In this passage, we find Obi sliding dangerously from his original lofty frame of mind. Obi's inflexibility toward the members of the Umofia Progressive Union was not motivated by simple pride; it was a noble attempt to guard his personal freedom. Obi should never have buckled under that type of pressure, because the attempt by his clan representatives to manage his life instantiated a vulgar power display, a denial of individual human freedom, of Obi's right to be an independent human being.

Any attempt to resist enslavement, any effort to gain one's liberty, any attempt to be master of oneself and to wriggle out of the degrading conrol of another power is an act of courage. Obi endears himself to readers when he announces how determined he is to take full control of his life. Teeming with anger and daring, he tells the members of the Umofia Progressive Union that he would brook no further attempt to curtail his personal freedom:

> 'I am not going to listen to you any more. I take back my request. I shall start paying you back at the end of this month. Now, this minute! but don't you dare interfere in my affairs again. And if this is what you meet about, he said in Ibo, 'you may cut off my two legs if you ever find them here again.' He made for the door. (75)

Since the narrative wavers in its presention of the Umofia Progressive Union, readers find it difficult determining whether to view it as a benevolent organization eager to give Obi a helping hand, or a malevolent one intent upon carrying out a vindictive campaign to destroy a kinsman.

One may see the Umofia Progressive Union as composed of many well-meaning individuals. In that case, their action shows how a supposedly harmless act (in fact, a gesture of goodwill directed to one of their own) produces adverse effects. For this miscarriage of altruism, one can hold the altered circumstances generated by the conflict of values responsible; the disharmony between African communalism and Western individualism. The essential humanity of the Union is even indicated by their concern for Obi's wellbeing. In the scene where the clan rallies together to offer Obi warm support, he is facing court charges relating to moral decline, and the group is aware of the potential risks to its public image. The action of the Union members reflects the resiliency of traditional African values. If they bother Obi, it is because they wish him nothing but personal victory. While colonialism has weakened many aspects of traditional culture, the sense of fellow-feeling, the recognition of the familial bonds within the tribes is one of the core surviving elements of African culture. The bond is especially strengthened under difficult circumstances like these.

In the narrative, the greatest challenge posed by colonialism is to traditional integrity. *No Longer at Ease* portrays corruption as so savage, it is inescapable. Corruption pervades all institutional structures, posing a real threat to the moral fiber of society. It is inextricably bound up with the conflict of cultures. That Obi does not grasp this shows how shallow-minded he is. Obi's limited view of his situation is most clearly brought into focus during the argument with his friend Christopher. Tracing the roots of the problem deep down to colonialism, Christopher is sympathetic to Obi's situation. He wants to help Obi understand these matters.

Christopher stands profoundly confounded, however, listening to Obi's attempts to blame the moral decadence on the wrong sources—on the symptons rather than the actual causes: the civil service and "these so-called experienced men at the top" whom Obi believes have "no intellectual foundations to support their experience." Here is part of Obi's explanation to Chris of the social malaise:

> 'But take one of these old men. He probably left school thirty years ago in standard six. He has worked steadily to the top through bribery—an ordeal by bribery. To him the bribe is natural. He gave it and he expects it. Our people say that if you pay homage to the man on top, others will pay homage to you when it is your turn to be on top. Well, that is what the old men say.'[12]

Obi's slowness of mind is traced to a process that has turned him into a detached, aloof, isolated, individual; one torn apart from his native culture. If the notion of bribery as a domain of "the old brigade" were true, it goes without saying that Obi himself, a youngman katapulted by a British university degree into a senior civil service post, would of course have been immune to it. However, as Obi learns the hard way, the corruption of Africans does not arise from innate deficiency. Rather, it flows from the irrepressible financial pressures embedded within the system.

Opening the narrative with Obi's trial helps readers catch a revealing glimpse of a highly visual scene that exposes Nigeria's corruption in all its complexity. The varied reactions to Obi's conviction project the well-defined racial divide in the country. This divi-

sion pitted whites against blacks. Thus, for Mr. Green, Obi's immediate white boss, Obi's action is quite in character. Green expresses
the conviction that "The African is corrupt through and through."[13]
However, the narrative lends greater credibility to the opposing view-
point held by the members of the Umofia Progressive Union, and it
has been confirmed that "The entire novel may be read as a refuta-
tion of Green's remarks."[14]

The members of the Union decide to call an emergency meeting in support of Obi, because they resent the whole incident, which
stands out for them in all its vulgarity as an illustration of their collective victimization. The president of the Union captures the mood
of the group by his witty counsel: "A kinsman in trouble had to be
saved, not blamed... anger against a brother was felt in the flesh,
not in the bone."[15] The foundation of the Union members' frustration must be properly understood. They are unequivocal in opposing corruption. Angered and revulsed by the cancer, they are also
dismayed by Obi's inexperience in dealing with it. Their ultimate
motive is to help Obi exercise his sense of good judgment:

> When the time for warning came the men of Umofia could
> be trusted to give it in full measure, pressed down and
> flowing over. The President said it was a thing of shame for
> a man in the senior service to go to prison for twenty
> pounds. He repeated twenty pounds, spitting it out. 'I am
> against people reaping where they have not sown. But we
> have a saying that if you want to eat a toad you should look
> for a fat and juicy one.'
> 'It is all lack of experience,' said another man. 'He should
> not have accepted the money himself. What others do is
> tell you to go and hand it to their house boy. Obi tried to do
> what everyone does without finding out how it was done.'
> He told the proverb of the house rat who went swimming
> with his friend the lizard and died from cold, for while the
> lizard's scales kept him dry the rat's body remained wet.[16]

The issue of Obi's corruption and his clan members' reaction has
drawn frequent comment. According to Innes, for example, the
group does not regard bribery as essentially wrong, what it condemns is Obi's inexperience in handling it.[17]

On the contrary, Achebe uses those proverbs evoking the evil of reaping where one has not sown, and the sickening habit of eating toads, emphatically to clarify how loathsome an evil the people consider bribery and corruption to be. These proverbs convey the people's desperation. Though they know it is evil, they have been compelled to regard corruption as an inextricable part and parcle of the civil service inherited from colonialism, which they feel they are helpless to change or to avoid in their present circumstances.

Ironically, by acquiescing so despairingly in their corrupt environment, the local people cause the law-enforcement agents who should enforce integrity, to take advantage of the apathy of the natives to perpetuate the evil that the law officers have been mandated to fight. In this way, the obnoxious practice becomes an established pattern of life. The novel portrays the native authority's failure to suppress corruption as a morally confounding cultural disaster.

THE ROOTS OF ALIENATION: MISSION-HOUSE UPBRINGING & EUROPEAN EDUCATION

Obi's most faithful friend Joseph once remarks that Obi is just a man made "stranger in his country [by] mission-house upbringing and European education."[18] There can be no better diagnosis of Obi's experience. The novel traces the cause of Obi's disinheritance to his hybridized upbringing in which Obi's parents, like Achebe's, have taught their young one to despise his native culture. While subjecting him to daily doses of the Bible, Obi recalls how his father had fanatically forbidden his wife to tell their young son folktales. "'We are not heathens,' he said.'Stories like that are not for the people of the Church'."[19]

After going through such an early system that suppressed his interest in traditional values, Obi is left with a cultural void that results in permanent feelings of personal inadequacy. Obi began to notice this personality defect early. At the elementary school, for instance, there is a particular lesson Obi can never forget. "It was called 'Oral'. During this period the teacher called on any pupil to tell the class a folk-story....Obi loved these stories but knew none which he could tell." One outstanding episode resulted in Obi's resounding humiliation in class:

One day the teacher called on him to face the class and tell them a story. As he came out and stood before them he trembled.

'*Olulu ofe oge*,' he began in the tradition of folk-tales, but that was all he knew. His lips quivered but no other sounds came out. The class burst into derisive laughter, and tears filled his eyes and rolled down his cheeks as he went back to his place.[20]

The implication is that the packaging of Obi's upbringing is, in fact, nothing more than a systematic process of cultural disinheritance, which his formal schooling only helped exacerbate. It has been observed long ago that

the racism and cultural boastfulness harbored by capitalism were also included in the package of colonial education. Colonial schooling was an education for subordination, exploitation, the creation of mental confusion, and the development of underdevelopment.[21]

Because he was placed in a context where peer valuation played a crucial role in building personality, when he proved incapable of telling a folk tale, the "derisive laughter" of Obi's class mates caused him an incalculable psychological injury. Obi's deepening self-withdrawal reflects his growing sense of inferiority.

METROPOLITAN VERSUS COLONIAL EDUCATION: SHATTERING THE CONSTRUCTIONS OF DIFFERENCE

No Longer at Ease does not give any special thematic prominence to the fact that Obi completed his formal education in England. Rather, it calls into question the sharp distinctions that people drew about the quality of colonial and metropolitan education in those early days of the contact with the West. During the prayer she says at Obi's send-off party, Mary, "one of the most zealous Christians in Umofia and a good friend of Obi's mother," expresses such a view when she makes the claim that England is "the place where learning finally came to an end."[22] Nevertheless, the narrative's major emphasis blurs such distinctions. Instead, the novel mainly shows England as the place that heightens the protagonist's sense of difference, increases his nationalistic sentiments, and deepens his nostalgic longing for home.

It was natural that Obi's love for his fatherland should grow in exponential relation to the growing hostility of his hosts. Obi recalls later one strategy he developed for coping with racism abroad: He spoke his mother tongue "whenever he had the least opportunity of doing so," because "nothing gave him greater pleasure than to find another Ibo-speaking student in a London bus."

> But when he had to speak in English with a Nigerian student from another tribe he lowered his voice. It was humiliating to have to speak to one's countryman in a foreign language, especially in the presence of the proud owners of that language. They would naturally assume that one had no language of one's own. He wished they were here to-day to see. Let them come to Umofia now and listen to the talk of men who made a great art of conversation. Let them come and see men and women and children who knew how to live, whose joy of life had not yet been killed by those who claimed to teach other nations how to live.[23]

This excerpt offers significant clues. It points to some bitter experiences in Obi's four-year stay in England. Although he obviously was subjected to experiences that emphasized the presumed inferiority of his race, the specific nature of those events is not featured in this novel. To be sure, Obi's current perspective and disposition would best gain significance when viewed within the specific context of the particular abuses he suffered abroad. This omission is one of the story's greatest flaws.

Divested of any other locus, England's most noteworthy role is narratological. It serves expediently as the main site, the location, for the chance meeting of Obi and Clara. Their friendship initially begins as a casual affair in a London dance hall, and then takes an interesting formal turn when the two meet again on a ship during their return journey to Nigeria. The contrast between Clara's sophistication and Obi's awkwardness, between his exceeding aloofness and her alertness, however, becomes immediately evident. Whereas Clara senses from the start the futility of their encounter, Obi believed he had a genuine passion, and he is confident of his ability to sustain it.

As it turns out, and one commentator has said, Clara is the greatest test on the quality of Obi's education:

> Obi's moment of crisis (and, therefore, of choice) arises from his association with Clara. To marry or not to marry an *osu*: that's the issue. While it must be admitted that Obi had faced problems before Clara's revelation of her ancsetry, it must also be admitted that these were problems of financial management which made no real demands on his moral center. Was he, after Clara's revelation, going to withdraw his promises of love and marriage because of a primitive and ill-conceived code of social stratification? Especially in the face of his education and supposed enlightenment?.... Clara's revelation becomes the point of decision and choice for Obi, the crossroads in their relationship and his life.[24]

If we discount the trifling of the financial pressures on Obi's moral frame—we have already stressed the decisive role of financial burdens in Obi's moral decline—one will not quarrel with that critic's interpretation of Clara's symbolism. In any case, it is indicated that had it not been for the anonymity fostered by the city, the association that eventually brings Obi and Clara much pain and sorrow would most certainly never have happened in the first place. However, following their inabilty to resist the appeal of companionate involvement, the couple should have found the courage to nurture their relationship. Through marriage, the couple could have shown that they are two mature individuals mentally capable of taking responsibility for their actions.

It is particularly ironic that Obi would simultaneously seek autonomy in some aspects of his life while accepting to be shackled in others. Obi should have never succumbed so easily to prejudice. He should have met his father's use of emotional tactics in defending bigotry with his own independent will or volition. It may be wise to absorb foreign influences with discretion; Obi's father shocks us by his inability to use the Christianity that he openly professes in a manner to solve, rather than to exacerbate, local problems.

I know Josiah Okeke very well.' ... 'I know him and I know his wife. He is a good man and a great Christian. But he is an osu. Naaman, captain of the great host of Syria, was a great man and honourable, he was also a mighty man of valour, but he was a leper.' He paused so that this great and felicitious analogy might sink with its heavy and dreadful weight.

Osu is like leprosy in the minds of our people. I beg of you, my son, not to bring the mark of shame and leprosy into your family. If you do, your children and your children's children unto the third and fourth generations will curse your memory. It is not for myself I speak; my days are few. You will bring sorrow on your head and the heads of your children. Who will marry your daughters? Whose daughters will your sons marry? Think of that, my son. We are Christians, but we cannot marry our own daughters.[25]

In theory, Obi's father recognizes the value of self-denial and is all too anxious to enjoin his son to make personal sacrifices in order to fulfil himself as an individual. However, when his own faith is put to the test, Obi's father essentially refuses to live by his word. Obi should have paused to question his father's use of biblical allusions to defend an un-Christian tradition. That attitude does not inspire one to regard Christianity as the liberational force the missionaries make it out to be. With greater power of independent judgment, Obi could prove wrong society's belief that being an *osu* is a stigma that not even education can help those so categorized to overcome. As Eustace Palmer notes too, this argument is premised on such wobbly points, with determination, Obi could demolish it quite easily. "Although his father expressed complete disapproval, it is obvious that he will be won over in time, since he himself was a rebel."[26] A person made of sterner stuff could easily have resisted all that gibberish from his father.

The emotional tactics employed by Obi's mother are even more pitiful. A true master of rhetoric, Obi's mother has a sound knowledge of the power of atmosphere. She admonishes her son to put his personal appetite last, for instance, encapsulating her admonitions in a recent horrifying dream.

'I dreamt a bad dream, a very bad dream one night. I was

> lying on a bed spread with white cloth and I felt something
> creepy against my skin. I looked down on the bed and found
> that a swarm of white termites had eaten it up, and the mat
> and the white cloth. Yes, termites had eaten up the bed right
> under me.'"

The dream, she goes on to explain, took on meaningful significance
when the letter from Obi's friend Joseph broke the dreadful news
of Obi's plans to marry an *osu*:

> 'I saw the meaning of my death in the dream. Then I told
> your father about it.' She stopped and took a deep breath.
> 'I have nothing to tell you in this matter except one thing. If
> you want to marry this girl, you must wait until I am no
> more. If God hears your prayers, you will not wait long.'
> She stopped again. Obi was terrified by the change that
> had come over her. She looked strange as if she had sud-
> denly gone off her head.[27]

Metaphor, proverbial usage, symbolical dream reference, and mi-
metic drama are the techniques that help ground the oral configura-
tions of the mother's speech. Obi's mother may understand well,
and may be even desperate, to take the fullest advantage of the
power of words accompanied with appropriate body movement;
words in the company of the right gestures. All the same, Obi should
never have been so naive as to be taken in by his mother's antics.

The inability to muster the courage to endow Obi with greater
nerve shows Achebe's bow to the pressure of conservative social
values. While the anxiety to do what is politically correct runs counter
to the role of teacher, Achebe is an artist who knows his purpose.
He should have braced up a bit and donned the mask of a rebel.
Achebe puts too much into the making of Obi that conforms to the
stereotypical notion that the Western-educated African is a victim
of unsuitable systems of instruction. Although there are instances
of Africans unnerved by Western education, many others gain
strength rather than weakness from their learning. We need to see
more of such exemplary figures in our fiction. To dwell exclusively
on weaknesses, on deficits, on what is lacking is to yield to a de-
spairing vision of the world. Obi's absolute gullibility is baffling.

There is an unwarranted absence of personal courage and vision in his composition.

By permiting such devious schemes to influence the dissolution of their engagement, Obi suffers a loss of no mean significance. He fails to see Clara as the real asset she is. Closely examined, Clara may appear not as much an individual human being as an emotional prop for Obi. Although an apparition, Clara's power is enormous. Whenever he is bereft of her, Clara's absence leaves Obi so completely lost he is unable to gather any coherence of meaning. Obi's inability to attend his mother's funeral in Clara's absence reveals how much he rests on her. Were it not for the loss of Clara, for example, Obi might easily have overcome the ridicule of his Lagos clansmen, who explain his situation in terms of being caught up by the Lagos mess—that is, alcohol, money, women, and life in the fast lane.

Just as too often happens, Clara suffers the fate of many great persons whose lives and contributions go unappreciated until crisis or disaster intervene. Obi just cannot make it without Clara. Corruption is floating in the air all over the country. In the absence of Clara's stabilizing influence, Obi is drained of his initial idealism. He takes advantage of the women who seek him out professionally. Obi's effort to stand up to the pervasive power of corruptive influences is undermined in part by his own underdeveloped moral sense. Obi does not fully understand his situation. That's why he is in part a victim of forces larger than himself. Ultimately *No Longer at Ease* ends as a study of the wreckage brought on by corruption. In the book, it is Obi and Clara who provide Achebe with an appropriate opportunity to explore his understanding of the travails and challenges the pioneer Western educated Nigerians faced.

Making a living during a transitional period in the life of any nation is an arduous undertaking, it is even more wearisome for people in formerly colonized territories. As Achebe's book indicates, every attempt these people take to achieve harmony in their lives is futile, foredoomed. Artistically *No Longer at Ease* is a very gripping novel. In it, Achebe succeeds handsomely in showing how the private spills into the public arena of our lives. Obi and Clara's efforts to achieve success either on the professional or the domestic front are frustrated by the contradictions that accompany the colonial encounter. Their frustrations bear unmistakable testimony to the mental and cultural dislocation colonial domination caused a generation of Africans in their own homeland. The exploration could acquire even greater resonance, however, if too much emphasis is not placed on human failure and more stress placed on the indomitable human spirit. *No Longer at Ease* is short on solutions. It diagnoses problems without showing the light that could lead out of the tunnel. Most accounts of the effects of colonial education weigh too heavily on the negative side and too little by way of remedy; yet education can be, and has served as, a means for empowerment. As Fredric Jameson has ventured, "fantasy or protonarrative structure [is] the vehicle for our experience of the real."[28] Because uncertainty and instability are bound to arise in any context of transition, for a writer to see beyond the gloom, to present a glimpse of paradise, project a way to attain it, is to claim his/her rightful place as a possessor of durable vision. This is something the author of *No Longer at Ease* doesn't do. Achebe's analysis in this novel is not inspiriting because he yields too readily to a presentation that leaves the educated African elite forevermore locked into the victim status—though we know that education can be a weapon for positive change.

POST-INDEPENDENCE DISILLUSIONMENT: SUBJECTS RAMPANT, REALISM VERSUS REPRESENTATION, THE FAILURE OF REALISM

There is a pervasive belief that colonization stripped the African of his character, of his innate integrity, of his essential being. This is the view explored in *A Man of the People*. It is a view that denies the role of human personal agency—the belief that individuals possess the power to determine their own destiny. In *A Man of the People*, a work that has come to be regarded as without a doubt Achebe's ultimate novel of post-independence disillusionment, Achebe obviously set out to outline and analyse the depressing political situations in Nigeria immediately after independence in the 1960s. Among African novels, no other work, except perhaps Ayi Kwei Armah's *The Beautyful Ones Are Not Yet Born*, has brought to the fore, with as much dramatic vigor, the problem of artistic representation in African literature; giving literary expression to an obviously painful truth without losing oneself to the sweep of emotion.

How can the writer balance patriotic fervor or politics with the technical demands of art or aestethic considerations? What is the sensible balance between reference and imagination, between fact and fiction? In *A Man of The People*, Achebe's choice is to work through a first-person narrator. Through the observations of his alter ego, Odili Samalu, the author plans to portray events he personally witnessed. The style meshes harmoniously with the narrative's goal to present idealism or the dream of personal freedom as Achebe's personal governing ideals that can be extended to the political terrain. Odili, a young university graduate, decides to become a teacher because he believes the teaching profession will best guarantee personal freedom.

Indeed, Odili is portrayed early in the work as a patriotic individual who knows his country well and who should provide a reliable perspective through which we can view events. Initially, the political campaigns of Odili's elementary school teacher seem the perfect opportunity to watch the behavior of his fellow countrymen closely. Despite the glamorous life of the political elite, Odili shows an educated awareness of, and aversion to, their dirty practices. Adding to the pathos of their situation are the rigging, violence, thuggery, deception, lies, manipulations, and bribery that Odili witnesses everywhere around the politicians. *A Man of the People* thus begins with gloomy observations.

Odili, however, is a sleazy creature, and his image as an anti-corruption crusader is not sustained for long. Degenerating into the habit of nagging irritably about the sweltering corruption, his emotional reaction to what he regards as the incompetence of the leadership denies him the clear-sighted ability to appraise the situation. His very first mistake is misreading the minister's handling of the inflation issue, which he sees as a reflection of the immutable contempt in which politicians hold the educated people. From his perspective, when the prime minister rejects the articulated package that minister of finance and reknowned economist Dr. Makinde prepares for dealing with the country's inflation, it is because politicians generally despise ideas. Not only are the minds of politicians ruled by political expediency rather than by sound common sense, the way the prime minister suppresses opposition further convinces Odili that his plan is to perpetuate himself in office forever.

A newspaper editorial damning the products of eggheads attests to the low regard people have for education.

> Let us now and for all time extract from the body-politic as a dentist extracts a stinking tooth all those decadent stooges versed in text-book economics and aping the white man's mannerisms and way of speaking. We are proud to be Africans. Our true leaders are not those intoxicated with their Oxford, Cambridge or Harvard degrees but those who speak the language of the people. Away with the damnable and expensive university education which only alienates an African from his rich and ancient culture and puts him above his people.[29]

An immediate problem is for the reader to discern whether this is an honest and well-meaning appraisal of the nation's situation or just a piece of sychophantic outburst that uses denunciations of the educated elite and appeals to the rhetoric of independence for self-serving ends. Politics is established right at the start as a means by which people clamber for access to materials, power, and ego. There is no mention of any exceptions—as there are bound to be—to the rule.

Since Odili hardly knows himself, he knows others even less. He suggests that traditional humanism has been eroded, that acts of any unselfish nature are out of the question. The prime considerations of people, he holds, are profit-oriented. The novel fails to anchor the truth claims of such an ominous pattern. Using the isolated action of Jonathan Nwege, the proprietor and principal of Odili's school, to prove political corruption at the grassroots oversimplifies issues considerably. Odili thinks that Nwege's ambition alone determines that educated people are greedy and are always eyeing material reward whenever they work.

Achebe delineates Nwege's ambition through his lingering hope that "something" will show up for him in the form of "old matresses, chairs, electric fans, disused type-writers and other junk which at present was auctioned by civil servants."[30] Since a proposed new corporation is taking over the disposal of all government unseviceable property, Nwege has high hopes that his dream will materialize. The fervor Nwege displayed at the rally organized for Nanga's campaigns is part of his effort to ingratiate himself with authority. It is a measure of Nwege's small-mindedness, according to Odili, that when he doesn't get the favors he seeks from the higher quarters, Nwege's disappointment turns into envy for those favored like Odili. Since Nwege considers people like Odili undeserving of such bene-faction, Odili's invitation to the ministerial lodge provokes his rage.

But Odili is unworthy of serving as the point of view for observ-ing and reporting events. He is prejudiced not only against Nwege but also the villagers, whom he dismmisses effortlessly when he describes their behavior at the rally arranged for Nanga's cam-paign at the Anata Grammar School. By denying the villagers them-selves a voice and a physical presence of their own, the narrative gives the reader a biased view of them, making the reader learn far less about the community than about the narrator—an opinionated, pompous, bigoted, and sneering figure. Here, for example, is a part of what the narrator says about the masses:

> As I stood in one corner of that vast tumult waiting for the arrival of the Minister I felt intense bitterness welling up in my mouth. Here were silly, ignorant villagers dancing them-selves lame and waiting to blow off their gunpowder in honour of one of those who had started the country off the slopes of inflation. I wished for a miracle, for a voice of thunder, to hush this ridiculous festival and tell the poor contemptible people one or two truths. But of course it would be useless. They were not only ignorant but cynical. Tell them that this man had used his position to enrich himself and they would ask you—as my father did—if you thought that a sensible man would spit out the juicy morsel that good fortune placed in his mouth.[31]

The failure to depict the villagers in their objective reality denies the readers the opportunity to see the villagers in their authentic exist-ence—independent of their representation by the narrator. They fail to come to life as flesh and blood humans, and fall short of our expectations of "characterizations of interest."[32] In other words, Odili fails to portray the masses as human figures who come to life as they respond with vision to their complex situation. Though por-trayed as ignorant, cynical, and timid, since the masses are not a physical presence in the novel—but are seen only through Odili's unreliable eyes—the narrative denies the reader an eye-witness account of a crucial piece of evidence. We the readers see little of the cultural habits of the people to justify Odili's low opinion of them.

Odili's gold-digging attitude makes Chief Nanga's theft of his girl friend serve as a deserved poetic justice. Out of generosity, Chief Nanga has opened the doors of his home to Odili. An unselfish leader, Nanga's original desire is to help the young man from his constituency take up "a strategic post in the civil service." Nanga's motivation is that his people "shouldn't leave everything to the highland tribes. Our people must press for their share of the national cake."[33] He wants his community to take their piece of the nation's wealth. This is what other groups in the country are doing, for all regard their nation as a gigantic resource that each of its components are in competition to extract as much riches from as they can in the shortest time-frame possible.

Early in the novel, the narrator articulates Chief Nanga's sterling qualities. He is portrayed as having warmth of character. Nanga rapports with people because he respects others, and he is generous with his wealth because he is clearly not in politics simply for personal gain. He himself tells his supporters, "I no de keep anini for myself, na so so troway. If some person come to you and say 'I wan make you Minister' make you run like blazes comot. Na true word I tell you. To God who made me ... Minister de sweet for eye but too much katakata de for inside. Believe me yours sincerely."[34] Achebe could not possibly deny positive attributes to Nanga because he is a product of his environment—rather than someone of inherent moral deficiency.

Hot for adventure, Odili profoundly enjoys the hospitality of the Nangas. While he finds Chief Nanga charming, he describes Mrs. Nanga as a warm, cool-headed, and generous hostess. A housewife, who considers the glamorous life within the elite circles a little bit insincere and tasteless, Mrs. Nanga is nevertheless open-minded enough to tolerate it with a sense of good-humored delight. Odili himself caused his disaffection with Chief Nanga, for it is his insincerity that mars his mission to Bori, the nation's capital.

The main reason Odili accepts the Nangas' invitation is the expectation of romance. Odili sees the Nanga's home as a suitable place where he can go to have a good time with his girl friend Elsie.

However, being the enemy of truth that he is, when asked to define the exact nature of this relationship, Odili lies to Chief Nanga that she is not all that important to him but merely a girl friend. Had Odili not given his host the wrong impression about Elsie—whom he describes as being nothing more than a libertine, freely seeking pleasure—Chief Nanga might not have been so readily encouraged to seek his own delectation with her.

All during the time Nanga is seducing Elsie, Odili takes no steps to stop him although he is evidently burning with anger. When Odili does act, it is vengeance he considers. Adewale Maja-Pearce puts his finger on the matter when he reasons in *A Mask Dancing* that it is revenge "rather than political conviction" that "propels Odili on a course of action, which is why his prime motive is not victory in the forthcoming election in order that he might serve his otherwise troubled country, but conquest of his enemy's fiancé, Edna, in order that he might salvage his otherwise shattered ego."[35] Thus, Odili's desire to get even with Chief Nanga by consorting with Edna, Nanga's second wife-to-be, stems from anger—an emotion seldom constructive. The ironies are bitter indeed, for it is difficult to understand why Odili makes no bones about committing adultery by hopping into bed with Jean, a total stranger—and a married woman for that matter—but should react with such moral outrage at Chief Nanga's date with a single lady like Elsie. Because it is the quest to avenge Nanga's seduction of Elsie that prompts Odili's participation in politics, rather than any noble vision of duty to the nation, Odili's political motivations seem frivolous.

Maja-Pearce goes on to observe that he finds an undecisive air in this novel; that the work is suspended on the brink of pornography. His view is exaggerated, especially when he concludes that "it might have been better for everybody concerned, not excepting the women, if the author had set out from the beginning to write a pornographic novel.... The result would have been a less dishonest book; or, at least, one which did not pretend to a morality it does not possess, such as Cyprian Ekwensi's *Jagua Nana* (1961), a much more convincing (and more vigorous) novel for that reason."[36] Maja-Pearce's discussion of this novel was generally sound and helpful to my argument; but I do not see the element of dishonesty or pornography in the text. Instead, I see a botched effort. *A Man of the People* is one of those experiments that don't quite work out. It ends as an artistic failure not because Achebe isn't faithful to his convictions, but because he employs the wrong artistic methods, devices that fail to help the writer in his laudable quest. Overall, the failure results from an inability to present an ironic structure of values in the text.

One of the ironies of the post-colonial African writing embedded in *A Man of the People* is that it is an exercise in contradictions. The novel marks an attempt to depart from the convention of expatriate writing of which especially Achebe's first novel, *Things Fall Apart*, and, to a lesser degree, his third, *Arrow of God*, are stark examples. To my mind, in expatriate writing, the native writer unwittingly perpetuates the imperialist stereotypes of the colonized he sets out to correct. As writing in which his primary market is the English audience, Achebe's expatriate writing sees him engaged in a fruitless game of defending to the aliens the nobility of his marginalized existence. Even though he himself has denied this, Achebe's expatriate style in his early novels can be decoded through the ceaseless recourse he made to the use of proverbs in his illusory agenda to authenticate the culture of the dispossessed. E. N. Obiechina notes, in another context, that proverbs are powerful cultural items, because they are kernels that contain "the wisdom of traditional people."[37]

In his early fiction, Achebe made abundant use of proverbs for a firm political purpose. Chantal Zabus, who has listed their occurrence painstakingly, for instance, observes of Achebe's most political early novel, *Arrow of God,* that it is "in Achebe's *œuvre* and possibly in the West African Europhone corpus of fiction, the novel which has the largest number of proverbs—a minimum of 129."[38] Unfortunately, despite the many insights it offers, the proverb cannot illuminate the national, not to talk of the continental, culture; and the value of the proverb in Achebe's early fiction is limited to the fresh views it offers on Igbo ethnic ways of life. Clearly the proverb is Achebe's most potent weapon in a tradition of writing, where, to borrow Daniel Corkey's words, he as a colonized person presents a discourse that seeks "to explain the quaintness of the humankind of this land, especially the native humankind, to another humankind that was not quaint, that was standard."[39]

In *A Man of the People*, Achebe aims to make his art more directly relevant to the whole African continent. Because his literary ideology derives from the belief (also shared by Fanon) that the primary goal of writing must be to contribute to the liberation of the nation through the recovery of its culture, he had to redefine the parameters of fiction.[40] This means that he had to remove his work from an Igbo ethnic domain, underscoring its continental applicability. Thus, we find Achebe in *A Man of the People* freeing himself from the convention of extensive proverbial embellishment in which his earlier fiction is mired not merely, as Zabus claims, to show "how the urban Igbo speaker is alienated from the traditional art of conversation and the proper use of proverbs."[41] More importantly, I believe the goal is to achieve the universalistic imperative, a concept to which Achebe himself objects.

Ironically, in an attempt to fill the gap created by the absence of proverbs, Achebe embarks on a project of narration that sees him taking firmer possession of the European tradition he wishes to abrogate—that of creating more introspective characters. By dwelling intensely on the workings of his characters' consciousness to the neglect of their social environment, Achebe creates a thin setting or background to their action. This is what E. N. Obiechina probably has in mind when he complains that in *A Man of the People* there is "little integration of setting with narrative and little use of it to further psychological insights."[42] The episode reporting the reception arranged for Chief Nanga's political campaign in Anata illustrates this. Another episode, which highlights the clumsiness of the narrative, is the scene where Odili meets the night-soil men who are clearing bucket latrines in the streets of Bori, the country's capital city.

When Odili confronts the slums in the city, Achebe's concern, as Rosemary Colmer points out, is "emphasizing Odili's blindness at this stage in the novel to the social issues which ought to concern an idealistic young politician."[43] The narrative focus is on the problems which are uppermost in Odili's mind, such as his sexual frustration. But the failure to play up the sordid element in his environment leads to an insufficiency in the representation of that which the ire of the idealistic young politician ought to be stirred against.

Because there could be no better way for a chronicler of the contemporary African experience to provide an in-depth analysis of the social malaise afflicting the continent than to give a mirror image of the social environment, an assignment that Achebe refuses to carry out, he makes the fatal mistake by employing the metaphor of a military coup (which he uses at the close of the novel) as a central symbol to universalize his story. Bernth Lindfors writes that he believes "Achebe ended the novel with a military coup in order to enlarge the picture to include Nigeria's neighbours, many of which had experienced coups."[44] According to Lindfors in the same article:

> By universalizing the story in this way, Achebe could suggest to his countrymen that what had happened in other unstable independent African countries might easily have happened in Nigeria too. The coup was meant as an African parable, not a Nigerian prophecy.[45]

For Lindfors, "the novel owes as much to what Achebe had observed in his own country." However, he fails to scrutinize the narrative strategies with sufficient rigor to convincingly show how a work, which lacks a dramatic *locus operandi*, can be applicable to "other independent African countries." In general, Lindfors's comments might be convincing as counters to the prevailing assumptions about the "prophetic" nature of Achebe's novel, but his overall assessment is not persuasive, for he is convinced that by "ending with a coup, an event anticipated yet still unknown in Nigeria but familiar elsewhere in Africa, Achebe added a dimension of universality to his story."[46] Pursuing an argument that calls to mind the debate questioning how a writer can best achieve universality—whether he can best approach it by rooting the experience in the local and concrete or suggest it in a generalized manner—Lindfors obviously endorses the generalist and abstractionist approach that Achebe adopted, which runs counter to the more suitable device of the particularistic sensibility.

Eric Heyne makes an observation that is extremely relevant in assessing *A Man of the People*, stating that "inaccuracy is not necessarily fatal to a nonfiction text; neither, of course, does accuracy necessarily guarantee a work of literature.[...] Moreover, there is never one version of any event that is best for all purposes."[47] With this in mind, it is pertinent to say that *A Man of the People* is not being assessed merely for tests of objectivity, but simply for the competent use of appropriate representational strategies that guarantees holding a compelling mirror of its material. Thus the objection raised against the manner of fictional representation in *A Man of the People* is that the narrative's disquisitions on Odili's consciousness throughout the novel might have satisfied what is clearly the author's long-standing interest in achieving character development by means of psychological realism, but they lead to sacrifices of opportunities to display a more intimate knowledge of the hero's outer world. Ultimately, the style fails to satisfy the reader who wants to see more of the environment in, and against, which the hero, as the novel's centering consciousness, acts out his role.

An aspect of contemporary African life often depicted in the African novel as a carry-over from the colonial era is the existence of inequality. The creation of social disparity is evident in the uneven distribution of social amenities between the members of the elite (who supplanted the erstwhile white overlords) and the exploited generality of Africans. In *A Man of the People* Achebe gives acknowledgment to this issue. However, the ambiquity in the response of his mouthpiece Odili Samulu leaves Achebe himself open to a charge of indifference. We learn, for example, that Odili is both "amused and surprised that in the capital city, Bori, the urban-poor can afford only to live in shacks, or sleep in the streets, and can only afford pails for the disposal of human waste" whereas in the "same city he finds out that the members of the ruling social group, such as Nanga, live in mansions with basic amenities."[48]

Finding amusement in the suffering of others is heinous. Chief Nanga's elephantic home (from the cosy comfort of which Odili indulges himself with a condescending attention to the condition of the exploited people) is a wasteful structure into which scarce resources have been diverted that could otherwise be used to improve the lives of the underprivileged. While reading newspaper reports of what he himself describes as "the cosy comfort" of Chief Nanga's "princely several bathroom mansion with its seven gleaming silent-action closets," Odili's playful comments about the squalid habitation of the poor capture Achebe's own sensibilities.[49]

Why does Achebe show disinterestedness toward such a serious problem? E. N. Obiechina, once again, surmises that it is because of "Achebe's own uneasiness in the Lagos setting." Obiechina explains:

> He had lived in Lagos, with only a few intermissions, be-
> tween 1954 and 1966, during his career in the Nigerian broad-
> casting Corporation, but it is likely that he never really got
> into the spirit and rhythm of life of that turbulent city. Lagos
> must have seemed to him, in his quiet, self-possessed, so-
> ber, introspective life, a threatening whirlpool round which
> it could be necessary to pick one's way cautiously to avoid
> being drawn in.[50]

Obiechina goes on to cite Cyprian Ekwensi and Wole Soyinka, re-
spectively, as examples of writers whose "outgoing temperament"
and "dramatist's cosmopolitan temperament prepared them to explore the physical realities of Lagos in a way which Achebe's more
retiring, introspective nature must have inhibited." Obiechina's argument is brilliant, starkly exposing Achebe's main limitation as a
writer using the realist mode.

To understand why *A Man of the People* mainly generates
doubt and distrust, we must go beyond the preliminary recognition
that its author is intensely aware of the power of narrative; we
must investigate his actual performance in the act of narration.
What this means is that we must answer the question: Why does
this work create such hesitation in the reader—despite the author's
keen recognition of the enormous role narrative plays, and despite
his presumed familiarity with the fictional material he employs?
The superficiality of insight into the game of politics and the lack of
positive response in terms of a vision of rebirth and renewal are the
major drawbacks of this novel.

THE RELIABILITY TEST: NARRATIVE PLOYS
Inappropriate narrative strategies also play a major part in undermining the impact of *A Man of the People*. The strategy, placing
reliance on the unreliable first-person narrator, departs dramatically from that employed in Achebe's earlier fiction, where the
omniscient third-person narrative ably highlights the worth of Igbo
tribal customs as well as the weaknesses that hastened their ero-
sion by Western values. In *A Man of the People*, the first-person
approach does not effectively meet the demands of commorative
accuracy. There is an absence of any intellectual or moral view-
point that we might expect for rigorously analyzing the situation at

hand. The goals of the earlier works necessitate objective methodology in order to balance admiration for both village life and the more healthy aspects of the "civilizing mission," unfortunately, the same technique of detachment, though largely appropriate for those novels of rural life, is thoroughly unsuitable for dealing with a corrupt present, since the latter situation now requires narrational strategies that might give direction to resolution of the impasse. Indeed, as Rosemary Colmer correctly points out, the problems involved in the adoption of the first person narrative point of view for the story of *A Man of the People* are compounded by the character of the narrator, Odili Samalu, because he "constantly vacillates between moral sentiment and underhand action, so that what audience sympathy he has is established by the narrative form, not by his firm stand for a moral philosophy."[51]

Why does the text favor the use of such a yarn spinner, someone who, in Biodun Jeyifo's words, totally lacks "positive currents of values, predispositions, identity"?[52] Why does Achebe depend on a narrator whose "uncertain posture," as Simon Gikandi reminds us, "questions the authenticity of the events presented."[53] Although nearly all its critics believe Achebe uses this structure in order to reflect the reality of the situation, there is disagreement about its level of success. G. D. Killam, for example, accords the text undue praise,[54] as does Lindfors in an article referred to earlier.[55] While a good number of critics recognize the flaws inherent in the text's structure, many are ambivalent in their overall assessment.

Thus Simon Gikandi, in his study *Reading Chinua Achebe*, is thoroughly exasperated by the narrative procedures. "Why does the narrative roam from one level to the other and how are we expected to explain all these movements in time and space?" he asks. Gikandi dismisses any idea that Achebe is out to "estrange his readers from the events narrated," arguing that "such shifts are intended to underscore the problem" Odili faces in coming to terms with the chaotic situation in his country:

> As both a character and narrator, Odili would prefer to fit the truths and realities of the nation—and Chief Nanga's place in the collapse of the nationalistic dream—into clear political, cultural and social categories, but the historical crises in the new nation negates this desire for systemati-

zation.[56]

Gikandi perceives tremendous growth in Odili in the process of the narration, in terms of his understanding "the gap that separates past ideals (the desire for change and transformation) with present realities(corruption and aggrandizement)." Gikandi, then, goes on to observe that at the end of the novel Odili's "knowledge and perspective" are still a long way from being "fully cognizant of the cultural patterns and traditional institutions which lead to the pitfalls of national consciousness." This not withstanding, Gikandi persists in the belief that the novel provides good answers to the dilemma, even though he never fully explains how the narrator's "ability to retrace the process by which the dream of national liberation was negated allows him to propose an ontological possibility for change and transformation." [57]

M. J. C. Echeruo articulates a similar equivocation. He attempts to show Achebe's use of the first person narrative as a determining factor in his success "in creating the necessary authenticity of narration" that gives "a further illusion of intimacy to the events being narrated." At the same time, Echeruo ties the novel's failure to the device. "*A Man of the People* is not Achebe's best novel," he intones, attributing its point of central weakness to "the moral character of the world of the novel....the absence of a system of accepted values by which the character of Odili or of Chief Nanga can be evaluated independently of history." As Echeruo correctly remarks on the same page, the novel's main defect arises from how "Achebe allowed himself a cynicism which did not permit him to invent such (accepted) values."[58]

The thesis of cynicism can be extended to suggest that Achebe's sympathetic handling of both Odili and (to a lesser extent) Chief Nanga indicates an uncertainty in his own values at this time. Dispirited by the depth of decay in the Nigerian society, the novelist's conviction of the ultimate triumph of honesty almost caves in. Achebe abdicates the role he himself envisioned for the members of his class in terms of teacher and path-finder. Odili's contradictions, which reflect his creator's, are evident when the reader juxtaposes his thoughts, motives, utterances, and actions with those of the figures he castigates. His visit to the Nangas, where he first tastes the richness of the politician's lifestyle, crucially highlights an important aspect of his personality. It is during this visit that Odili has an opportunity to make some of his most penetrating attempts at explaining the malaise attacking the nation, but the value of his comments is totally undercut by his fascination with the luxurious comfort of the palace. Charmed by the opulence of his new surroundings, Odili confesses that if he had the chance to be a minister he would want to remain one for ever. He explains:

> A man who has just come in from the rain and dried his body and put on dry clothes is more reluctant to go out again than another who has been indoors all the time. The trouble with our new nation—as I saw it then lying on the bed—was that none of us had been indoors long enough to be able to say ' To hell with it'. We had all been in the rain together until yesterday. Then a handfull of us—the smart and the lucky and hardly ever the best — had scrambled for the one shelter our former rulers left, and had taken it over and barricaded themselves in.[59]

This passage clearly exposes Odili's moral crisis. In using poverty as a justification for the African politicians' compromise of their integrity, he lowers himself to the rank of the corrupt politicians whom he criticizes. Clues about Odili's decision to participate in politics later are here. Chief Nanga's theft of his girl friend Elsie is only the immediate context precipitating that decision.

A Man of the People is marked with an obsessive interest in mapping the psychological horizon of the hero-narrator Odili Samalu. One of the telling revelations is Odili's conscious desire, driven, as it were, by a passion to take Chief Nanga's full identity. Odili's desire is to have the power to command others and to will his aspirations into existence. He would like to inspire fear and respect in his compatriots. This dream surfaces most explicitly during his ride to visit Elsie in the politician's chauffeur-driven Cadillac. Describing his sense of elation in that brief moment of power, Odili tells us:

> In our country a long American car driven by a white-uniformed chauffeur and flying a Ministerial flag could pass through the eye of the needle. The hospital gateman promptly levered the iron barrier and saluted. The elderly

male nurse I beckoned to had sprinted forward with an agility that you would think had left him at least a decade ago. And as I said earlier, although it was against all the laws of the hospital, they had let me into the female nurses' quarters and woken up Elsie to see me.[60]

Given Odili's exultation at the red-carpet treatment and his contempt for the underprivileged, Gerald Moore is correct in his observation that "Achebe's strategy is to show us a young man who is potentially another Chief Nanga himself (though of a more recent model)."[61] Driving has, since Achebe first used it here, served as an unflattering symbol for portraying the ostentation of the African politicians. The long car, probably as an element Ayi Kwei Armah borrowed from Achebe and then transformed into his own in *The Beautyful Ones Are Not Yet Born*, is a striking symbol of affluence and corruption that is seen as draining the resources of the nation that could otherwise be more profitably invested elsewhere for the benefit of the majority.

If the symbolic place of driving is in some way curious in *A Man of the People*, this has more to do with the problems the novelist encountered in inventing narrative strategies to give form to the experience. The fault lies, specifically, in the overdose of humor in Achebe's satiric armory, which leaves what ought to be biting rather muted. The car metaphor specifically deserves attention. It is connected with the overall absence of any durable vision of alternative societal values. Colmer is right: What goes wrong with Achebe's novel is its inappropriate narrative strategy and characterazation:

> He [the narrator] approves of his past idealism, but laughs at his own naivety. He invites us to admire his prowess, both as speaker and as lover, and his recognition of his own craving for admiration does not lead him to any radical reappraisal of his own self-concept. He is honest enough to let the truth appear to the reader, but not honest enough with himself to change his concept of himself. The most important change in him is his recognition of the importance of honesty and integrity in the individual, coupled with his new understanding of what it means to be 'a man of the people', but these are not enough to prevent him, by

the end of the novel, applauding murder as an unselfish act
and embezzling party funds. [62]

It is the same quality that leads Eustace Palmer to describe the
book as "that rare bird in the corpus of African literature—a comic
novel."[63] The narrator's slangy language, replete with clichés and
commonplace idiomatic expressions, reflects Achebe's playfulness
throughout the novel. This unexpected blemish persists even in the
much discussed matter of Odili's break with Nanga and the series
of actions he contemplates while in hospital at the end of the novel.

ANTHILLS OF THE SAVANNAH: STRUCTURE OF DISORDER

In *Anthills of the Savannah*, his fifth-published and latest novel,
Achebe writes ably about the governing ideas and the practices of
military dictatorships in Africa. The work gains supremely in immediacy and realism. The fictional land of Kangan, where the story
is set, is a country at the mercy of a ruthless dictator. Achebe's
picture of patronage and cronyism gives the reader a glimpse of
what happens when office holders are picked not because of their
personal merit but because of other factors completely unrelated to
entitlement. Achebe dramatically draws up the pattern of misrule
through the collaboration of political stooges. The unfolding scenes
of dictatorship enact a depressing situation.

In a word, since all the key members of the cabinet have to
recommend them for their positions is their connection to Lord
Lugard College (all were former schoolmates of the Head of State
there), the future implied is a world that would continue to be ruled
by what the novelist terms the perfected "art of flattery" disguised
as "debate." The sycophancy surrounding the leadership is portrayed by that macabre scene in which the Chief Secretary is ar-
ranging His Excellency's shoes. We see how intimately conjoined
the day-to-day happenings are. Closely linked to the leadership's
ineptitude, the inability of the regime to lead the country effectively,
is the situation where workers like the Chief Secretary get ahead
primarily by good reading of their master's moods. For the military
regime, time is so hopelessly taken up with managing crises in the
cabinet, the leadership has very little time left for actually running
the nation itself. Achebe suggests that the calamity facing the nation can be explained primarily in terms of a leadership problem.

Achebe defined this theme earlier in his political pamphlet *The Trouble with Nigeria*, but there he gave the topic only a brisk dramatic representation. *Anthills* is a new contribution. It addresses the leadership problem with a more steady and elaborate unfolding. Its impact derives in part from clear analysis. The problem of leadership is compounded by inadequate succession methods, for it is individuals who are all too willing to be agents of oppression and those people who cannot be expected to be instrumental in bringing about any level of revolutionary change who are often favored in appointments to serve in advisory capacities. What lends *Anthills of the Savannah* additional poignancy is that it carefully knits together imagination or ideology and historical actuality. Both are processed in this case in the framework of ideas held about human behavior; first-hand observations of living in Nigeria during the 1980s.

In *Anthills of the Savannah*, Achebe finally comes to a full understanding of the problems involved in allying realism with left-wing political creed. In facing up to the difficult task of meshing calm reflection with enthusiastic political analysis, he somehow finds the means to resolve the conflict between these contradictory elements, always in contention in a ferocious struggle for prominence. To come to *Anthills of the Savannah* with expectations of socialist realism is to be disappointed. The narrative not only keeps its formalistic elements in check; its ideology is tilted more to the side of reform than revolution. To some readers, then, the book might appear an ambiquous project, since it does not follow through with the formal demands of the Marxist class analysis within which the novelist chooses to place it. The question of how to marry aesthetics and ideology coherently is always paramount in narrative. In *Anthills*, Achebe creates entirely new ground for discussing the question of dogma within the context of narrative. The presentation, whereby he views the failure of the educated elite to respond to the needs of the masses as a performance qualifying them to be described as the new colonialists, serves as a good occasion for underwriting the power of satire. His handling of his central theme, investigation, is particularly apt. He presents us with a memorable cast of characters. In this parade, Professor Okong, a droll figure stands out as a major player who best exemplifies Achebe's deft imaginative prognostication.

Because it is self-interest rather than patriotic call to duty that motivates Professor Okong (the exemplum image of the political leadership) to seek authority in the first place, the narrative gains immense power as it paints his picture. Here is an individual whose career is dominated by a nefarious desire to hold on to power in perpetuity. So desperate is he in his ambition, Professor Okong's anxieties are demonstrated by the only clothes he wears—"khaki safari suits complete with epaulettes"—clothes that show his eagerness to ingratiate himself with the military authority.[64]

Okong's military outfits are not only odd; they are outrageous. Though named Commissioner for Home Affairs, in truth, Okong knows anything except the happenings around him. Okong emerges as one of the most revolting figures of political corruption portrayed in African fiction. He allegorizes one of the painful ironies of post-independent Nigeria, because his grooming stands out perfectly as a miniature image of the distorted values on which the nation's elite sustains itself. The product of Baptist Missionary training, Okong gains his elevation through the mentoring of Chris Oriko (during the latter's tenure as editor of *The Gazette*, the nation's paper). Okong's meteoric rise serves as a classic illustration of the dangers of cronyism, for he is a person without creativity who has not earned his position. Okong's writing for the national paper, as Chris recalls later, is "full of cliché."[65]

In several crucial passages of *Anthills*, Achebe delineates Okong's launch into the limelight, into an environment thoroughly ensanguined with stupidity. Loyalty is a value missing in Okong. The one thing is certain: For Okong, personal interests are constant, though his political allegiances are forever shifting. To serve his own wretched motives, when Okong senses power slipping out of the politicians' control, he quickly turns into their bitterest critic. In so doing, he effortlessly wins the friendship of the military, the new power brokers. One of the abiding facts of Okong's political life is never forgetting to whom he owes his current position. Used to terrifying acts of sycophantic homage, Okong is willing to sink to any level. Manipulation, intrigue, and opportunism are Okong's defining qualities. The narrative attributes the Okongs' pranks in the system with the inefficiency, senseless hate, animosity, rank opportunism, and the reckless display of power and wealth that typify its culture.

THE ESSENTIAL CHARACTER OF A GOOD LEADER

Anthills of the Savannah definitely addresses one of the main areas where questions have been raised in several studies of Achebe's fiction: the claim that he takes minimal interest in, or even makes total ommision of, offering any vision of how Nigerian society in particular (and Africa in general) can emerge from the problems that corrode its body politic. However, in continuing to chart the story of Nigerian people's growing complicity in their own destruction, Achebe's elaborate effort in *Anthills* to depict some role models is a welcome point of departure. The creation of these figures suggests Achebe's new-found optimism, evinced in a new approach to fiction. He extends his vision into the future with hope, depicts proggressive roles for women and the youth, who are, up to this point, two of society's least liberated groups.

Anthills shifts at least from a state of trepidation—if not entirely from despair—to one of expectancy; it presenting women as a real source of opposition for the military's regime of terror. It parades women whose self-assurance rubs off on the men in their lives. The novel's protagonist, Ikem, for example, owes a lot to womanhood. Ikem's case highlights the personal sacrifices needed to move the nation forward. Achebe casts Ikem as a person who challenges orthodoxy. Though he winds up paying the ultimate price for his courage, the lesson of Ikem's action resonates. By giving due acknowledgment to the difficulties Ikem faces, Achebe lifts the narrative from the domain of naive idealism.

Ikem has been described as an "example of an African deeply involved in the intellectual project of postcolonialism"; someone thoroughly "gripped by doubts about his own notions of self, community, and social purpose."[66] His true nature emerges and in devoted service to his community, the Abazon folk. Ikem pursues politics with a selfless passion. It is ironic that the same passion would lead to his termination as editor of the nation's newspaper and to his eventual murder.

Bumpy as the road is to freedom for Ikem's people, Ikem leads them with single-minded dedication. In their effort to contain the intolerance of the military junta, the community sends a delegation to the nation's capital with one agenda—to protest the state of its dismal neglect. The people want to ease the poverty threatening their survival. His Excellency's regime is suspicious of the move because its abiding philosophy is that "petitions and demonstrations and those kinds of things are sheer signs of indiscipline. Allow any of it, from whatever quarter, and you are as good as sunk."[67] With surprising ingenuousness, or rather with the insensitivity of a caliber expected only of its kind, the regime suppresses the delegation of these honest, dedicated, and law-abiding citizens.

The reason Ikem is made the immediate scapegoat and held accountable for the legitimate yearnings of an entire community is most bizarre. The ruthless action of those in power may reveal an arrogance reminiscent of the disdain with which a colonial order carries out its activities; but the abuse from the new rulers is especially intolerable. Coming, as it does, from fellow compatriots, the dishonor betrays the yearning of the people that independence will not ony restore material abundance but also autonomy and dignity denied by colonization. By acting out of the notion that the people do not have the initiative to take decisions for themselves, the indigenous authority shows its contempt for those under its command. The regime argues that without insipiration from educated upstarts like Ikem the community would never have risen from aparthy on its own. It is this thesis that the regime uses as an excuse for unleashing its repressive measures on the activists, exposing the panic that revolutionary ideas engender on authoritarian administrations intent upon maintaning the status quo.

Achebe is most commonly known for his use of culturally authenticating material in his fiction. In *Anthills*, he shows a newfound willingness to experiment with psychological realism. This pays off handsomely, particularly, his use of Ikem's consciousness as a basis for conducting a subtle investigation into the background of Sam, His Excellency. In his report, Ikem has the privilege of conferring an informed and compassionate understanding rare in narrative. Right from the start, it is clear that Ikem should know Sam intimately. Not even Sam's crises of identity can elude Ikem. Ikem has known Sam right from his days at Sandhurst, Britain's general military academy.

In one of his most finely tuned presentations, Achebe shows that Nigeria misplaces priorities by sending her sons to Sandhurst. Not only does the training take a great deal away from them, it inadequately prepares them for leadership. Impoverished of any leadership qualities he originally possessed, Sam, worse still, is also deprived of the political will needed to select capable hands that could assist him in government. The result is a profound uncertainty. Kangan's experience can stand specifically for Nigeria and generally for any other African nation. The events are duplicated everywhere on the continent. Ikem's analysis is compelling. His voice is devoid of Odili's egotistical tone, the cardinal defect of *A Man of the People*.

Sam's ever-readiness to put the interests of foreign partners before those of his nation is one of the greatest banes of his administration. That, too, is replicated continent-wide.

> To say that Sam was never very bright is not to suggest that he was a dunce at any time in the past or that he is one now. His major flaw was that all he ever wanted was to do what was expected of him especially by the English whom he admired sometimes to the point of foolishness. When our headmaster, John Williams, told him that the Army was the career for gentlemen he immediately abandoned thoughts of becoming a doctor and became a soldier. I am sure the only reason he didn't marry the English girl MM found for him in Surrey was the shattering example of Chris and his American wife Louise.[68]

With these few remarks on neo-colonial tentacles, we have ample enough proof to show that the individual who now leads the black nation called Kangan is a person who even regrets the fact of being black. We ask: How can such a person successfully lead a nation which he is yet to show positive identification with?

Sam's friendship with the English character known as John Kent, alias Mad Medico or MM, most clearly portrays the role which hate of country can play in alliance with international interests in sabotaging the national aspirations of formerly colonized countries in general. John is a bumpkin, a former pimp, but he exercises a weird clamp on the African leadership. John's role is a sad comment on the sexual predilection of the man who has since become the head of state. The control is suggestive of the general difficulty the new nation is facing in its effort to break free of the authority of its former colonial masters.

That everyone in authority continues to consider John indispens-able, even though his lack of qualifications is widely acknowledged as well as secretly discussed in black leadership circles in which he moves, is perplexing. Both in the figurative and the literal sense, John's position as the gate-man in the life-line of the country dem-onstrates clearly the extent of the reckless disregard the regime holds the health of the nation. Why has such an unqualified indi-vidual been given leadership of the Ministry of Health, undoubtedly one of the most pivotal sectors of the government?

It is fitting that the two people most vocal in their opposition to the misrule—Ikem and his girl friend Beatrice—serve as represen-tative voices through which the narrative best articulates the evolv-ing political and aesthetic convictions of the author. Both stand out in their entire society as inflexible defenders of morality. Ikem and Beatrice are unrelenting in their opposition to both the repression of the indigenous ruling elite and the selfish acts of incendiary foreign collaborators like John Kent. Ikem and Beatrice seek the total eman-cipation of their country from every form of external manipulation, exploitation, and oppression. The former appears more credible because his creator, like most male African writers, does not know enough about womanhood to be able to overcome stereotypical depiction of women.

AN UNEASY DIALECTIC:
WORD VERSUS ACTION AS WEAPON

Achebe's portrayal of Ikem marks a great advance in his narrative style. With Ikem, Achebe takes another step in his search for liter-ary techniques most effectively to convey ideologically charged ideas. Initiated by Marx in *A Man of the People*, the style has come full cycle with the creation of Ikem in *Anthills of the Savan-nah*. Ikem operates on a level which is at once deep and profound. Chris's aspiration to similar heights may collapse on a pathetic note (he discredits Ikem's work and ideals as futile, escapist, and ro-mantic—a judgment not endorsed by the author).

Ikem has realistic goals for his community. His aspirations for his people are basic and do not require any heroism to attain. First, he wants to clear the people of their mental blockages. He begins with the issue of public executions. When one poor person is being killed in cold blood, Ikem seizes the opportunity to raise the issue for public debate. At the beach, other poor people are rejoicing, watching one of their own executed for having stolen a small amount of cash. Ikem talks about the injustice of the law. It is a system that victimizes poor people, he explains. Most of them steal for survival, and, when caught, they pay with their lives; but the rich who plunder the government coffers, not only do they get away with bigger crimes they are hailed for it by the same poor people, who are indifferent to the contradictions within the system. Ikem wants to educate poor people so that they can understand what is really happening to them.

Critics of Achebe's works argue that he identifies with the position of the Abazon elder. They misunderstand the whole debate. Achebe is not insensitive to the issue of the competing claims of action and word receiving national priority. The old man of Abazon says that the word (storytelling) is more important than anything else. Ikem disagrees with that. He believes the two—word and action—must work together to produce good and balanced results. When we read *Anthills of the Savannah* with care, we see that Achebe can't possibly disagree with Ikem. It cannot be for nothing that Achebe jeers at the old man's speech, which is too long for anyone sitting at one place to tolerably listen to. African people in general, and Igbos in particular, can tell good stories but even among them it is not a standard practice for the story-teller to dominate an entire session all by himself, like the old man does.

People who sermonize as the old man does may be suffering from the disease of loquaciousness—a common affliction of old age, which many elderly people have in villages all over Africa. Those types of "blabber-mouths" are hardly ever among the most reliable people in any society; there is no good reason to believe that Achebe would give them a significance so out of proportion with reality. True, the old man does ganeer a few proverbs in his narrative. However, in fact, *Anthills of the Savannah* negates the expectations of the way an Achebe novel reads in terms of stylistic uses of proverbs. Linguistically, *Anthills* is not a typical Achebe novel. It would be more appropriate to regard the old man as a comic parody of a tradition now nearly moribund. On this level,

Anthills of the Savannah shows that Achebe is absolutely honest with himself. Since there are no places in Africa where proverbs still occupy the distinguished official position they once held in the past, to give a contrary impression is to falsify reality.

Connected with the issue of integrity is the novel's portrayal of Ikem, who is not a superman but an average guy, like most. He may understand some things more clearly than others, but he is not special; quite unlike the idea of the hero Aristotle envisioned long ago. Ikem's relationship with the two taxi drivers is proof that he sees himself as a normal person. When they come to honor him, Ikem discourages them. He doesn't fool himself that he is poor like them; but neither does he see himself as superior to them. He knows it would be a lie to change from who he is all of a sudden and attempt committing class suicide.

The one thing Ikem knows for certain is that he can help everyone who crosses his path. Be they ordinary workers and students, or celebrities, Ikem believes he can reach out to everyone. Relative to Achebe's earlier protagonists, Ikem is in a class by himself. He comes into his own when he gives a lecture at the university. There he speaks in simple language that is accessible to everyone. He is persuasive. Loaded with apt examples, Ikem's language is at once clear and impassioned. His speech, which could appropriately be described as a "political meditation on the imperative of struggle,"[69] demonstrates the ability of the spoken word to inspire others to do something concrete in their lives.

In this lecture, Ikem explains why he believes the government is afraid of the people who tell stories. It is with the example of the influential storyteller from Kangan that Ikem buttresses the points of his argument. That the government sends this person to detention is important, for it shows that people like him "threaten all champions of control, they frighten usurpers of the right-to-freedom of the human spirit—in state, in church or mosque, in party congress, in the university or wherever."[70] On another occasion, Bassa Rotary Club, he surprises everyone when he attacks situations that make it necessary for some people to be donors while others remain receivers of benevolence. Though this is an audience least disposed to receive such a blow, Ikem boldly throws a challenge to these rich men who have come together at a luncheon celebrating their donating a water-tanker to a dispensary located in what is described as one of the poorest districts of the region, "an area t has never had electricity nor pipe-borne water."[71]

There are some minor contradictions in several aspects of Ikem's ideas, each of which confirms that in this novel Achebe is not interested in the perfect leadership image, one that might represent an ideal but would be unattainable in the real world. Thoroughly human, Ikem's imperfections reflect our own. That Ikem cries out against the expectation that writers provide answers to every problem facing their nation, for example, while he himself is very forthcoming with such answers, shows the absence of any form of self-congratulatory air. This is the attitude that the narrative urges African leaders in general to emulate in turn.

It matters little that Ikem's articulated program of mass enlightenment, which he calls "a new radicalism,"[72] does not much differ from the ideas of Karl Marx. Ikem is striving to induce everyone in his society to look inward at him/herself. He is recommending an approach to nation-building that emphasizes self-examination rather than blame on external forces. This is his attempt to wrest Africa from its traditional victim status. Ikem discourages self-immolation and urges society to come to terms with the reality of fraud, deceit, and dishonesty which are the governing ideals of the elite. Remarkably, at the same time, he encourages the masses to do battle with the greatest sickness they have, the ignorance confining the rank and file to their lowly station.

Because he does not entirely discount the roles such external influences as foreign capital and imperialism play in the wreck of Africa, Ikem performs a balancing act by becoming the voice of realism. Identifying aberrations like religious extremism, intolerance, and political thuggery as divisive tactics employed by the elite to maintain their strangle-hold on power may not seem particularly radical. However, Ikem's cold-blooded murder shortly after this lecture evinces both the callousness of the regime he exposed and the real dangers perennially facing those who attempt to unmask clandestine, powerful groups.

In its plotting against Ikem, the regime bears testimony to the desperate tactics to which the military can resort in its bid to perpetuate itself in power. When the regime fails in its attempt to use Chris as an instrument to victimize Ikem, the Head of State turns to a fictitious fellow, hastily designated the Chairman of the Board of

e *National Gazette*, who bears the signature of the
ation sent to Ikem. Why, the reader must ask, does
lie before Chris can re-define his whole career?
)wn senseless death at the end of the novel really
apart from adding romantic flair to the whole concept of
martyrdom? Perhaps the melodramatic portrayal of Chris shows
that in *Anthills of the Savannah* Achebe does not see creative
writing's value as residing primarily in its aesthetic considerations,
but rather in its ideological significance. The example of committed
literature is in its message, which should assist the liberation movement. The determined action, which Ikem's death inspires in Chris
(as he rallies the support of the foreign media and other opinion
moulders such as students as well as workers in protest of Ikem's
murder), might seem improbable, but its value lies in the lesson of
its gesture.

WOMEN'S NEW NATION-BUILDING EFFORTS

Achebe is constantly criticized for misrepresenting women's issues. Critic Patricia Alden does not believe that *Anthills of the
Savannah* departs considerably from the Achebe canon in regard
to his conceptualization of women. After giving a detailed critique
of hero Ikem's machismo, noting his disrespect of women, Alden
discusses at length the character of Beatrice, the principal woman
activist in the novel. She concludes that, even in this novel, Achebe
still "betrays a significant failure of imagination—a failure to take
seriously, as part of contemporary political struggle, the feminist
challenge to patriarchal authority, and a corresponding failure to
create convincing, interesting women characters."[73]

Quite outanding among the weaknesses Alden identifies is
Achebe's conflating the identity of Beatrice with the personality of
a mythical figure, which enables him to present Beatrice as a living
embodiment of "the water goddess Idemili, as Mother Africa."[74]
The basis for some of her objections to the gender distinctions in
the novel are not quite clear: Why, for example, she sees Beatrice's
holding "a responsible position in the government" but claims she
appears "largely restricted to the role of girlfriend"; and what is the
point of objection that Beatrice's author "names her as 'girl' in
contrast to the 'men' who are her contemporaries and friends to

Elewa"?[75] What is wrong with defining a woman through roles encompassing but not limited to her professional identity?

Since allegory is a tricky device to handle in a novel, the writer who wishes to use it successfully must use it with care. This is why the point also should be conceded to Alden that Achebe's use of allegory in *Anthills of the Savannah* is not entirely refined. Beatrice is not sufficiently individualized. It is distinctiveness that gives allegorical portraiture the edge. There is an attempt to root Beatrice within a concrete social milieu (see her lengthy monoloque, referenced on p. 12). So marginalized is Beatrice's individuality that her appearance is shadowy. More significant, though, is her role as narrator. Beatrice, a woman plays the crucial part of a key teller of tales for the first time in Achebe's major fiction. She executes her function so effectively that, in retrospect, we see what the preceding novels would have gained with the talents of a similar yarn spinner.

One feminine attribute that enhances Beatrice's performance is articulateness. A university graduate with a degree in English, Beatrice is exceptionally expressive. Articulation might not appear to be an essentially female attribute, but Beatrice's self-assurance gives a peculiar edge to her persuasive delivery. Chris notices this distinction when he first meets Beatrice in England. While he finds her performance in bed poor, he nevertheless enjoyed her company, primarily because of her linguistic skills. Sensitive and tender, Beatrice brings a feminine point of view that serves as a useful compliment to the dominant male attributes in this novel.

Of all of her attributes, none serves her so well at the dinner at the presidential retreat as her articulation. When this intelligent woman receives the invitation to the dinner, an invitation His Excellency himself describes as "something important and personal,"[76] her initial speculation is that she is being called upon by the Head of State to play a mediatory role in the conflicts of the men in power. At the party, she discovers that this isn't quite the case, and, instead, she has been invited in recognition of her other qualities—to showcase the nation's achievements to the world. Since Miss Cranford of the American United Press is in Bassa "to see if all the news they hear about us in America is true,"[77] Beatrice is deserving of the invitation. The solicitation recognizes Beatrice's talents that none other than Sam himself describes as phenomenal as she is clearly "one of the most brilliant daughters of this country"—a lady who made a first-class honors degree "not from a local university but from Queen Mary College, University of London."[78]

For Beatrice, though, what the occasion does present is the chance to address a number of concerns that she has never had the opportunity, up until then, to speak about publicly. First, is the matter of the political elite's appalling misbehavior, particularly the eagerness with which they court the approving eyes of Westerners. It bothers Beatrice that her country has given an unknown female American journalist (on some kind of tour) easy access to its number one citizen. While poverty and starvation ravage the general population, the foreign expert is encouraging the country to "maintain its present....levels of foreign debt servicing currently running at slightly more than fifty one percent of total national export earnings."[89] Thus, the claim to monopoly of wisdom and to ideas of nation-building expressed by the visiting American journalist conflicts with the interests of the state. Here, Beatrice is discussing a very fundamental problem: the reliance on a foreign model that perpetuates notions of Western cultural superiority that results in reckless importation and the abandonment of local initiative. Rather than expressing anti-American sentiments, she is deploring her country's inability to exercise its power of democratic sovereignty to decide its own destiny.

Patricia Alden has described the dinner party as a "trivialized ... arena for sexual combat," adding that she believes Beatrice "has been invited there merely to provide the 'woman's angle' for a visiting white female American journalist."[80] Commenting specifically, on the episode where Beatrice "first snubs, then attacks" the visiting white woman's position on foreign debt and the special attention the Head of State is giving her, Alden says:

> In this scene the cheapening of Beatrice and her association with the goddess comports oddly with the seriousness with which both are presented elsewhere. If her feminist consciousness and race-consciousness are meant to be interestingly at odds in this scene, this contradiction is not developed, nor elsewhere alluded to; thus important issues serve as the occasion for a farcical peek at Sam's

gigantic erection, atBeatrice's bumps and grinds.[81]

On the contrary, I believe the occasion juxtaposes Beatrice's good citizenship with the Head of State's inconstancy. It is disconcerting that Beatrice, an ordinary citizen, can see through the motives of a visitor who gives her host country advice she definitely knows is wrong, whereas the so-called number one statesman is too blinded by a lust of an essentially sexual nature. With that sort of "expert" advice, the visiting American demonstrates that she is far less concerned about the interests of the nation to which she has come ostensibly as an advisor on foreign affairs than she is in protecting vested Western assets in the region. Achebe manages the scene pretty well; though there is a melodramatic quality to Beatrice's case, there can be no doubting its wisdom or the nobility and genuineness of her intentions.

DEPICTING REALISTIC WOMANHOOD OR STEREOTYPE?

Turning to the reason Achebe is far less successful in his depiction of the female characters in the novel, it should be stressed in the strongest terms that there is nothing essentially wrong with the idea of men seeing women in their roles as either girl friends or mistresses or mothers, and so on. This is the way many men understand women. More important is the question: How do the women come off in these roles? The roles of girlfriend and mother are very important and needed roles, and women should take every pride in playing these roles. Furthermore, what women have a right to demand is to be represented authentically and realistically in the customary roles—whatever these are—and writers owe women an obligation to do so. Therefore, the relevant question is: How does Achebe fare within these parameters? Do his women act credibly in their assigned roles? Seen within such a context, Beatrice emerges much too much as an abstraction, a bit too much of an ideological tool. The relationship between Beatrice and Chris doesn't seem right. Why does Beatrice stay with Chris for so long when their relationship doesn't promise much, especially when there is little prospect of a lasting commitment? Similarly, the reader might ask: Why do Chris and Ikem remain lukewarm for so long?

If Achebe is aware of the African reality, he has given no inkling of it in depicting these relationships. The family remains a primary institution in Africa, where, unlike the West, marriage is its most basic stabilizing agent; demonstrations to the contrary in a novel that seeks to provide a living account of the contemporary African situation are misleading. While the relationship between them literally hangs in the balance, the lack of any substantial interest Chris shows in Beatrice is cruel, because she is totally devoted to him and deserves better. Chris is portrayed as lacking even the normal male instincts. This is demonstrated, for example, by his cool reaction to the news of Beatrice's invitation to the state dinner at the presidential retreat, to which Chris betrays none of the possessiveness many other men would show in a similar circumstance.

No, it isn't merely out of absoluteness of trust that Chris simply advises Beatrice to "keep all options open."[82] His coldness betrays more of indifference than trust. Days later, when Chris hadn't shown any interest or concern, Beatrice has to reprimand him:

> ... Chris you are behaving very strange indeed. Listen, let me ask you a simple question, Chris. I am the girl you say you want to marry. Right? OK, I am taken away in strange, very strange circumstances last night. I call you beforehand and tell you . You come over here and all you say to me is: 'Don't worry, it's all right'.[83]

Because Beatrice is not unaware of the importance her society attaches to marriage (she herself quotes approvingly the dictum, "better an unhappy marriage than an unhappy spinsterhood; better marry Mr. Wrong in this world than wait for Mr. Right in heaven"),[84] her decision to hang out for so long with a person who promises so little is baffling. The narrative has glaring difficulty bringing to life Beatrice and Chris' relationship. That Chris was coming out of a six-month marriage when he met and fell in love with Beatrice, whom he regarded as a very welcome change, should have been a good reason for tying the conjugal knot early.

Moreover, one can hardly find partners who are more fitting. Both are independent feminists who hit it off instantly. Chris himself acknowledges that:

> Beatrice is a perfect embodiment of my ideal woman, beau-

tiful without being glamorous. Peaceful but very strong. Very, very strong. I love her and will go at whatever pace she dictates. But sometimes I just wonder if I am not reading her signs wrong; if as MM says, without fully intending it, I have become too wizened by experience; if I have lost the touch, so to say.[85]

Chris is aloof and selfish, and he shows all the wrong emotions. His response contradicts all of his claims. Over this relationship, Achebe fritters away ideas with enormous potential for creating one of the most outstanding couples in African literature. It does not fit the emotion displayed, that Beatrice wants to regard Chris as considerate and compassionate. What this relationship does enact is a temporary union of convenience, for we see little sense of any genuine warmth of affection radiating through their treatment of one another. The novel fails to contribute any genuine images of love, for though Beatrice is constructed as a saint, her image, like Chris's unto his death, reveals inept characterization as well as absence of controlled plotting.

Even in the most promising union between a woman and a man in this work—that of Ikem and Elewa, which produces a child, the symbol of human regeneration—the traditional expectations and ideas of family and of relationship based upon social class of couples have been so fatally undercut, it is so ludicrous, for it denies the work any semblance of cultural validation. Elewa's transformation from pick-up girl to that of the mother of Ikem's daughter is quite unpolished because the distance between the educated elite and the masses makes it less likely that they would cross each other's path. So, while Ikem's association with this illiterate girl might be consistent with his depiction as someone who challenges convention, their relationship fails to come alive beyond the level of ideas.

So far as *Anthills of the Savannah* seeks eradication of the oppression, injustice, corruption, and indolence that have escalated in Africa since colonial occupation, however, its goals are not very different from those of any number of the younger African novel— Armah's *The Healers*; Ousmane's *Xala*; or Iyayi's *Heroes*. Nonetheless, whereas Armah, Ousmane, and Iyayi recommend radical solutions through armed resistance, reform of the existing order is Achebe's preferred solution. The works of all these writers thus bear witness to marked ideological differences. For attaining their ideal world, Armah, Ousmane, and Iyayi often draw lessons from the anticolonialist armed struggle on the continent with the satiric butt in their characterization, narrative design, and imagery shading off as a rule into open sympathy with the oppressed. On his part, Achebe, in his most recent novel, focuses on the period of black governance that he dissects with a sense of clinical realism. One goal that unites all the generations of African writers is restoring harmony, egalitarianism, political freedom, and material prosperity for all Africans.

Chapter 4

THE POLITICS OF STORYTELLING

Like many other creative writers from Africa, Achebe made his writing debut with the short story form, a convention that unquestionably has proven to be Africa's most effective counter to the imported narratives. However, the reason he did not consolidate his efforts within the short story goes hand in hand with the general disdain with which the short story is held by critics of modern African writing. Wilfried Feuser puts the case in perspective when he laments in his *Jazz and Palmwine* that critics of African writing have "paid scant attention to the short story and have treated it as a footnote to the novel" although "it is bursting with life." The short story has proven itself the form upon which an alternative tradition could be built, but Africans have neglected—if not abandoned—it entirely, undoubtedly because the prize for fiction has traditionally gone to the novelist, whom Feuser suitably terms "the long-distance runner" while the short story writer or "the sprinter" is cosigned to obscurity.[1]

Numerically Achebe's showing as a short story writer may not quite place him at a par with that of other world-class writers. Edgar Allan Poe, Nawal El Saadawi, Alex La Guma, Herman Melville, Nurudin Farah, Nathaniel Hawthorne, Buchi Emechetta, Anton Chekhov, Bessie Head, Henry James, Najib Mahfuz, James Joyce, Nadine Gordimer, Salman Rushdie, Albert Camus, Ama Ata Aidoo, William Faulkner, Gabriel Marquez, F. Scott Fitzgerald, V.S. Naipul, Richard Wright, Dambudzo Marechera, Margaret Artwood, Jamaica Kincaid, Ngugi wa Thiong'o, and Ernest Hemingway all not only distinguished themselves as master novelists but were equally at home in the terrain of short fiction. However, Achebe's effort is quite commendable. Despite its scantiness, Achebe should take solace in the very high quality of his output.[2] Achebe's stories merit attention not only because of the thematic links they bear with his longer narratives, but also because of the range of stylistic experimentation they put on display. In this chapter, I analyze Achebe's only book of short stories *Girls at War and Other Stories* (1972) to argue that all of his narrative experimentation in his short fiction can best be appreciated in the context of a debt to the oral tradition. Even the casual reader of Achebe's stories soon becomes aware of the reciprocal relationships that he strikes between his shorter and longer narratives. Though all his stories appear to move away from the direct communal concerns of the longer narratives, this is not really the case. In most of his stories, Achebe uses the experiences of individuals to explore the problems of the larger society. And so, ultimately, the stories constitute precious documents which portray socio-political, cultural, and economic changes of the community.

While growing up in the village of Ogidi in Eastern Nigeria during the 1930s, Achebe heard tales told both in the home by the fireside and in the wider community, for traditional storytelling flourished in the home as well as in the schools.[3] As noted by Isidore Okpewho in his important book *African Oral Literature*,[4] though different storytellers have different performance styles, there are certain resources which all performers have in their repertoire. Among these are repetition, tonal variation, parallelism, piling and association, the direct address, ideophones, digression, imagery, hyperbole, allusion, and symbolism. In addition, traditional tales tend to end with a moral appended to them often to confirm the norms of the society in which they are performed. Of these, the direct address (which ensures interaction with the audience), digression, exaggeration and didacticism are the features most prominently deployed by Achebe in his short stories. Though traditional storytelling influenced Achebe's short stories as much as—if not more than— it did his novels, this fact has surprisingly escaped the notice of his critics. Even more astonishing is the fact that some critics have made an effort to deny Achebe's oral heritage entirely. Among them is his long-time associate Ossie Enekwe, who claims that Achebe "developed as a writer in an environment where the short story form is not taken seriously, where there was no flourishing tradition of short fiction."[5] By arguing that Achebe "developed as a short story writer through dint of hard work and perseverence," Enekwe seems to excuse the presumed lack of short fiction in Achebe's oeuvre by blaming the unfavorable background in which Achebe grew up. Nonetheless, Enekwe's allegation that Achebe "made mistakes," that "these were steadily and systematically eliminated as he perfected his skill"[6] is unwarranted; such special pleading sweeps aside not only the fact that the Igbos generally hold storytelling in high regard, but also the fact that the art of storytelling can legitimately be taken as Achebe's greatest literary influence.

Achebe takes his heritage seriously. Even when the subject of his stories is slight, he is always able to capture the reader's interest with reasonable storytelling skills, as the first story of the collection "The Madman" (1972) clearly illustrates. In that story, Nwibe, an enterprising and eminent middle-aged man is about to take the Ozo title, one of the most prestigious awards in his community, when he suddenly experiences a reversal of fortune. His plight resembles Okonkwo's in Achebe's novel *Things Fall Apart* (1958), for, like Okonkwo, whose ambition to become one of the most respected elders of his community is ruined at the time he is about to achieve his goal, Nwibe's aspiration is thwarted at the most unexpected moment.

Indeed the destruction of Nwibe is rendered particularly poignant because he is able and determined to take full control of his life. Nwibe's quest for personal rejuvination by bathing at a local stream on his way from the farm turns out to be the occasion for his ruin. A naked madman, who had gone to the stream to drink water, spots Nwibe's loin cloth, gathers it, wraps it around his waist, and speeds away with it. Nwibe's attempt to retrieve his stolen loin cloth results in a chase that leads him to a market where on-lookers view his nakedness as a sign of insanity. Odun Balogun argues that the "involuntary but tragic exchange of identities between a sane person and a madman, an exchange symbolized by clothing" provides an appropriate occasion for a didactic lesson about life's "uncertainties."[7] As Balogun adds revealingly, "[t]he situation whereby a sane person is identified and treated as a madman not only underscores the precariousness of the claim of every sane person to sanity within the society, but also pinpoints the basic subjectivity of existence and human judgments. In fact, we cannot be sure of anything... But perhaps what the story has done is to equate extreme anger with insanity."[8] What should be added here is that the dilemma of Nwibe reflects the repercusions that follow when society assigns individuals to categories and, on that basis, determines whom to include in and whom to exclude from political, social, and cultural activities. Thus, Nwibe's plight, like Okonkwo's, stands as a dazzling metaphor for Africa's cultural dispossesion. The madman's posture at that significant moment in Nwibe's life and personal/psychic development makes pointedly clear the devious impulse of the attacker. "The madman watched him for quite a while. Each time he bent down to carry water in cupped hands from the shallow stream to his head and body the madman smiled at his parted behind. And then I remembered. This was the same hefty man who brought three others like him and whipped me out of my hut in the *Afo* market."[9] The stalking, deceitful actions that precede the madman's theft of Nwibe's cloth is reminiscent of the calculating actions of the colonialists who pounced on Africans at their least suspecting and most vulnerable moment to insure the success of the mission of colonial conquest.

In the following two stories "The Sacrificial Egg" and "Chike's School Days," Achebe employs oral literary devices in a way to meet different needs. Both stories continue to develop the theme of the unpredictability of life. Irony is an essential feature of both stories, and the crisp, direct, short sentences contribute immensely to the build up of the emotions explored in the pieces. "Chike's School Days" is especially remarkable for the economical, but effective way it evokes the reversal of fortunes brought about by colonialism. "Chike's School Days" depends for its effect on the use of digression, rumor or heresay, summary recapitulation, and authorial commentary, all of which are devices favored in oral storytelling, as they lend liveliness and a sense of immediacy to the events enacted.[10] The plot of the story focuses on the experience of Chike, an only son in a family of six children. The story begins as a study of Igbo cultural values, which reveals the craving Igbos have for male children and the joy that Chike's birth brings to his particular family. It then shifts to the ravages unleashed by colonialism. Chike was originally born an *Osu*, a member of families usually looked down upon in traditional Igbo culture. In relating the ferocity with which Chike snobs playmates from non-Christian families, the story pinpoints the terrible cultural consequences of the European colonial take over. The world brought into being by the extension of European rule was unjust. Instead of bringing about the equality Europeans claimed, their rule replaced one evil with another, for, in place of privilege and respect determined by birth and age, colonial rule super-imposed rank or social standing based on assimilation of the cultural model of Europe. Christianity and schooling were not only the primary institutions of Europeanization, but also of entitlement and social status. That reversal of fortunes does not present a viable solution to the problem of bigotry; this is why Achebe makes an allegorical representation of a successful marriage between a free-born and an *osu* a reality in this story, thus making it an important update on the novel *No longer at Ease* (1964),[11] where the attempt to achieve such parity had resulted in a disastrous failure."Chike's father was not originally an *osu*, but had gone and married an *osu* woman in the name of Christianity. It was unheard of for a man to make himself an osu in that way, with his eyes wide open. But then Amos was nothing if not mad. The new religion had gone to his head. It was like palm-wine. Some people drank it and remained sensible. Others lost every sense in their stomach." [12] Although the attempt to communicate a sense of those ostensibly attractive features of the new religion that hastened the supplanting of the indigenous culture of the Igbo by colonialism is a troubling throw-back to the liberal ideology of Achebe' novels, the story as a whole is definitely less tedious to follow.

In "The Sacrificial Egg," a more fatalistic story, there is a similar display of narrative eloquence. The story deals with the psychological and physical toll exerted on people by a small-pox epidemic in an Igbo town, Umuru, in the 1920s. To emphasize the power of supersition and to create an atmosphere and fear and helplessness, the people in town believe that the deadly epidemic is the handiwork of a local deity, Kitikpa, who is angry with the community. Achebe's interest, however, is the plight of an individual within the context of a general calamity: "Julius Obi sat gazing at his typewriter. The fat Chief Clerk, his boss, was snoring at his table. Outside, the gatekeeper in his green uniform was sleeping at his post. You couldn't blame him; no customer had passed through the gate for nearly a week. There was an empty basket on the giant weighing machine. A few palm-kernels lay desolately in the dust around the machine. Only the flies remained in strength."[13]

One of this story's intentions is to demonstrate what appears to be a conspiracy between colonialism, human failure, and nature in instigating the suffering of a community. The protagonist, Julius, is a Standard Six certificate holder, who works as a clerk in the offices of "the all-powerful European trading company which bought palm-kernels at its own price and cloth and metalware, also at its own price."[14] To the economic exploitation his community suffers in the hands of the imperialists, is added the scourge of the small-pox, which, we learn, not only killed its victim, but also "decorated"[15] the survivor.

The town itself has evolved from a small rural setting to a suburban locality, and with that have come a number of petty crimes and the fear of the ghosts believed to haunt its big market. However, the thrust of the story is the tragic encounter of the protagonist with a deadly destiny through a doomed love affair. When Julius seeks the hand of Janet in marriage, he receives her mother's support because of his Christian bearing. On a fated day, however, Julius and his girl friend part under foreboding circumstances. Julius is returning home in the night when he suddenly steps on a sacrificial egg. "In his hurry he stepped on something that broke with a slight liquid explosion... Someone oppressed by misfortune had brought the offering to the crossroads in the dusk."[16]

In a story dominated by traditional fatalism, there is an indication that one's destiny cannot be averted; this is why, despite Julius's firm attachment to the tenets of Christianity and his conviction that his education has freed him from traditional taboos, he seems to end up a victim of diabolic forces. Shortly after he breaks a sacrificial egg, his girl friend and her mother become afflicted with the deadly small-pox virus. The reader may feel that while the breaking of the egg may be a sign, a narrative device of foreshadowing and a reminder of Julius's or the town people's superstition, it is not the cause of the small-pox. However, for the actors in the story, there is a cause and effect here.

"Uncle Ben's Choice" develops the theme of destiny a step further by depicting one man's unsuccessful struggles to exist in a permanent state of innocence. The protagonist, known simply as Jolly Ben, works as a clerk in a trading company in the same locality as in the earlier story—Umuru—where he faces many temptations, among them alcohol and women, which are in plentiful supply. It is his choice, however, to remain a decent, responsible, and cautious man, and to live according to the injunctions laid down by traditional wisdom. If "Uncle Ben's Choice" stands out as a story, it is due to its use of the first-person narrator, which foreshadows the style of *A Man of the People* (1966),[17] a novel with which the story shares many thematic overlaps, including the elements of exaggeration, sustained reminiscence, tongue-in-cheek jollity, and riotous humor. In the opening paragraph of the story, the narrator sets the tone by establishing many layers of information. The narrator makes it clear, for instance, that he possesses some privileged historical information and that his decision to live frugally is not taken on account of being disadvantaged or lacking the resources necessary to sustain an indulgent life-style. He could afford to live on the fast-lane but he has chosen not to; his moral frame seems to suggest that his is the voice of the past's wisdom. He is an old man who can pass over the temptations of life with a wealth of experience behind him.

In particular, Ben recalls how he exhibited a special guarded behavior toward women. Even though he held a special attraction for them, unlike the hedonistic Odili Samalu in *A Man of the People*, Ben believes women are perilous: "The women of Umuru are very sharp; before you count A they count B. So I had to be very careful. I never showed any of them the road to my house and I never ate food they cooked for fear of love medicine. I had seen many young men kill themselves with women in those days, so I remembered my father's word: Never let a handshake pass the elbow."[18] The eventual termination of Ben's long-standing struggle for everlasting innocence is presented as measure of the inherent evilness of the city, whose degraded life is a threat to the permanence of traditional values. It happens that on a fateful New Year's Eve, there is much festivity everywhere and Ben momentarily relaxes his guard. "I had one roasted chicken and a tin of Guinea Gold. Yes, I used to smoke in those days."[19] In the early hours of that morning, Ben jumps on his new Raleigh bicycle and rides it home; when he gets straight to bed, "too tired to look for my lamp,"[20] but there he finds on his bed a woman whom he believed to be Margaret, his only female acquaintance: "So I began to laugh and touch her here and there. She was hundred per cent naked. I continued laughing and asked her when did she come. She did not say anything so I suspected she was annoyed ... I was still laughing when I noticed that her breasts were straight like the breasts of a girl of sixteen or seventeen, at most." It is stated that Ben was alarmed by the texture of her strange hair, which was "soft like the hair of a European."[21] This is why he jumps out of the bed, asking the lady to disclose her identity and threatening to strike a match. Before he can seek help from his neighbor Matthew Obi, however, Ben passes out and he has to be revived with cold water, without finding out who the woman was. He is told he has been visited by a Mami Wota or the fairy woman.

As in a typical oral storytelling performance, "Uncle Ben's Choice" ends with a moral lesson that is to reinforce the traditional values of the tribe. Despite the temptation to sleep with the Mami Wota in order to get rich quick, Ben recovers his guard because he would not give up his power to make and bring up children for material possessions. The lesson is driven home powerfully with the anecdotal story of Dr. J. M. Stuart-Young, who is remembered for having chosen to reverse the traditional wisdom: "For where is the man who will choose wealth instead of children? Except a crazy white man like Dr J. M. Stuart-Young. Oh, I didn't tell you. The same night that I drove Mami Wota out she went to Dr. J. M. Stuart-Young, a white merchant and became his lover. You have heard of him? Oh yes, he became the richest man in the whole country. But she did not allow him to marry. When he died, what happened? All his wealth went to outsiders. Is that good wealth? I ask you. God forbid."[22] The logic here is that Igbo (African) culture is people-centered and places primacy upon the value of children, as opposed to European culture which is materialistic or acquisitive. "Uncle Ben's Choice" ends as an exploration in which African humanism triumphs over acquisitiveness and other temptations of the city that came along with European influence.

All of Achebe's short stories stress the importance of ancient cultural traditions and habits in the survival and organizing of indigenous societies. This is evident even in early and amateurish pieces such as "Akueke" (in which the experience of a proud girl who refuses all suitors in the neighborhood serves to accentuate not only the primacy of marriage as a traditional institution but also the importance of family and of values like compassion and love) and "Marriage is a Private Affair" (which questions the custom of arranged marriage by exposing the prejudice against inter-tribal marriage and calls for tolerance and understanding in order to protect the institution of marriage which forms the bedrock of society). It is also evident in "Dead Men's Path" (a story employing the overzealousness of a young headmaster to teach basic lessons in moderation) and the stories "The Voter," "Vengeful Creditor," and "Girls at War," which focus on contemporary society, where corruption is pervasive, and in which the author attributes the malaise to the repudiation of traditional values that once cushioned people from moral depravity and the crisis it inevitably inflicts.

The life of Rufus Okeke in "The Voter" provides an apt occasion for an examination of the debility eroding the moral foundation of society. An energetic and hardworking young man, Rufus is unlike other people of his generation. He has made an early determination to resist the pull of the cities and has decided to remain in his village instead. By presenting the eventual corruption of Rufus within the context of an obsessively acquisitive, materialistic society, Achebe condemns the foreign influences which have effectively eroded traditional integrity. When Rufus is hired to direct the political campaigns of the Honourable Minister Markus Ibe, he has no divided allegiance. Rufus eventually deviates from his high moral principles when he notices politicians using their offices mainly for personal material gains. So pervasive are the abuses that the villagers are no longer taken in by the deceptions: "The villagers had had five years in which to see how quickly and plentifully politics brought wealth, chieftaincy titles, doctorate degrees and other honours some of which, like the last, had still to be explained satisfactorily to them; for in their naivety they still expected a doctor to be able to heal the sick. Anyhow, those honours and benefits had come so readily to the man to whom they had given their votes free of charge five years ago that they were now ready to try it a different way."[23]

The villagers' response is to put a price on their votes. In one of the most chilling political corruption documented in African fiction, they haggle over and over with one of the politicians' campaign managers. Despite Rufus's commitment to his moral principles, he ultimately succumbs to the corruption embedded in the system. The method by which he responds to the challenges facing the situation of not being able to be bound by one's word, not being able to honor it, or to be as good as one's word, foregrounds the state of desperation to which the well-meaning individual is driven by such a system. He cut his voters card into two and cast each half for the two candidates that he has been made to commit himself. By this act, Rufus attempts to achieve two goals simultaneously: to insure his self-defense against the *iyi* charm to which he had sworn while receiving a bribe from Markus's opponent, and at the same time to assuage his conscience that he did not really betray his friend. The use in modern politics of *Iyi*, "a fearsome little affair contained in a clay pot with feathers stuck into it,"[24] deployed to harm anyone who collects a bribe but renages the oath taken to vote for the giver of the bribe, reflects how desperate the politicians themselves have become; they are prepared to employ any immoral means that can lead them to victory because the stakes are exceptionally high for while the winner takes everything, the loser gets nothing. But, ironically, while the political elites exert enormous pressures on the masses to keep to their promises, the elites themselves do not show such exemplary behavior in their own conduct.

The inability of African leaders to keep their political promises is without question one of the reccurring themes of African writing. The story "Vengeful Creditor," however, is unique. It allows the reader a penetrating look into the world of political corruption and social neglect from the standpoint of ordinary people, thus confirming the notion that Achebe uses the short story to write for, and speak to, the people. Though not written in the language of the people, the story's accessability is bound to appeal to those ordinary Africans who have neither the lessure nor the skill to read elongated prose narratives like novels."Vengeful Creditor" achieves several goals simultaneously: it exposes the ostentatious life style of the elite and shows that it can be sustained only by corruption; it documents the failure of African governments' social policies; it explores the vested interests of powerful commercial concerns, revealing how they discourage genuine involvement; and it uncovers the hypocrisy of greedy political leaders, who take undue advantage of the masses.

"Vengeful Creditor" is a sophisticated, well-organized story revealing much structural coherence. Mrs. Emenike, the story's protagonist, is portrayed consistently through details which reveal that she takes the services she receives from her underpaid employees for granted. Achebe shows her in a shopping spree to bring out her individualistic personality and life style which is representative of her classs. Her arrogance is evident in her imposing demeanor, her superior airs at the cash counter, as well as in the shabby treatment she metes to the forty-year old "boy" whom she pays three pennies for carrying her purchases to her waiting car outside the shopping center.

The maliciousness of a master and mistress who lead their ward to the path of believing in promises they have no intention to keep is exposed in the story of Veronica, "a little girl of ten" whom the Emenikes have enticed away from her widowed mother so that she could serve them. Veronica dutifully and reliably serves the Emenikes. However, her boss and mistress refuse to honor their pledge to send her to school. Veronica is increasingly frustrated. She expresses her frustration in subtle songs of protest, but the Emenikes choose to view her songs in terms of their entertainment value as lullabies. Veronica then resorts to little acts of cruelty against the child under her care, ultimately giving the child ink to drink in a last desperate effort to avenge her maltreatment. It is easy to see that Veronica's action expresses a worthy but misdirected rage over being denied access to education. Indeed, during the confrontation between her mother and Mrs. Emenike, Veronica's mother puts her daughter's anger in clear perspective: "And that thing that calls himself a man talks to me about the craze for education. All his children go to school, even the one that is only two years; but that is no craze. Rich people have no craze. It is only when the children of poor widows like me want to go with the rest that it becomes a craze. What is this life? To God, what is it? And now my child thinks she must kill the baby she is hired to tend before she can get a chance. Who put such an abomination into her belly? God, you know I did not."[25] After listening to Veronica's mother voicing her concerns about the fate of her daughter living under the bad influences of Mrs. Emenike, Mr. Emenike mischievously admits that Veronica is "learning fast" and asks "Do you know the proverb which says that when mother cow chews giant grass her little calves watch her mouth?"[26]

Fortunately, Veronica's mother does not just express these apprehensions concerning child care and the danger of living under bad influences. The best solution, she thought, was simply to take back her daughter. This is probably the most salient moral adumbrated by"Vengeful Creditor": The belief that, just as power corrupts easily, slipping as readily into the lives of those who wield it as into the minds of those who are the victims, so subjugation can easily be transformed into a desire for retribution in the subjugated people.

Like "Vengeful Creditor," the collection's title story, "Girls at War," is also a tale of aborted human dreams, in which Achebe explores with moving honesty the repercusions on people of human greed within the context of war. "Girls at War" combines sensitivity, compassion, and clear-headed observation in presenting the corruption experienced during one of Africa's most destructive and senseless civil wars—the Nigeria-Biafra war of 1967-70. In it, Achebe captures a view of and presents the war as a machination of the elites, who profit so much from the ravages of society that they want it to go on indefinitely. In a manner reminiscent of Wilfred Owen in his war poems, Achebe juxtaposes the resignation of people with the determination of others who profit from the tragedy of victims.

The amoral relationship carried out between a Biafran officer Reginald Nwankwo of the Ministry of Justice and a vivacious and beautiful girl named Gladys, who works in the Fuel Directorate of the Biafran army, allows readers to gain an insight into the details of life during the war. Both Reginald and Gladys relate their own stories, divulging the degree of discomfort they feel about the social malaise in which they are caught, a decadence that seems to have eroded the very fabric of society. Nwankwo specifically holds women responsible for the decay. The story's title, which is taken from a comment made by Nwankwo about a girl friend of Gladys's, indicates the ironic distance with which the author views Nwankwo's position. The rumors being peddled by neighbors about the trips which Gladys's girl friend repeatedly makes to spend weekends in Liberiville in the company of her boy friend has provocked Nwankwo's comment that "She [Gladys] will come back on an arms plane loaded with shoes, wigs, pants, bras, cosmetics and what have you, which she will then sell and make thousands of pounds. You girls are really at war, aren't you?"[27] The comment is unfair since Nwankwo himself is equally guilty of profiteering from the war. In any case, Nwankwo's observation regarding the character of Gladys refutes his biased explanation of the situation.

Glays's beauty is so startling it gives Nwankwo the impression that "she had to be in the keep of some well-placed gentleman, one of those piling up money out of the war."[28] Her behavior is also consistent with his description of her as "a girl, who once had such beautiful faith in the struggle and was betrayed (no doubt about it) by some man. . . out for a good time."[29] Nwankwo distinguishes between those who exploit the war situation as a tactic for survival and those who are so perveted and lacking in ethical values that they take delight in making material gains from the death of others. However, events in the story indicate otherwise: Even Nwankwo's own experience tends to lend support to the hypothesis that people are not doing bad things because they are evil, but rather because they have to do what they need to survive. Nwankwo sympathizes with the poor and is never so happy as when he can distribute food to them. Ordinarily, Nwankwo would not want to steal from the masses. However, when the circumstances force him, Nnankwo diverts "tins and bags and cartons" of food supplies meant for distribution to the public to help in the upkeep of his own family while "starved crowds that perpetually hung around relief centres made rude, ungracious remarks."[30]

In his short stories, Achebe has shown that art can deal with trying moments like colonization and war and their aftereffects, that art can emerge from moments of utter chaos. One might legitimately say that Achebe has used art to represent or throw light on these circumstances. That he succeeds so well, especially in his short stories, in illuminating the circumstances shows remarkable powers of imagination. War—any war—whether waged against one by one's own relations or by outsiders; whether motivated by territorial greed or by ethnocentrism, is the most obvious indication of human life gone awfully wrong. This, surely, is the message of Achebe's stories. The generation that witnessed both the colonization of Africa and the Nigeria-Biafra War certainly knew the pain that resulted; reliving a sense of what it meant for the ordinary person to live through those circumstances is the major contribution of the few short stories Achebe has composed. In these stories Achebe has responded with sensitivity to the suffering of others. It can be argued that the quality of Achebe's short stories makes up for the lack of quantity. However, considering that Achebe has drawn his greatest strength as a creative writer primarily from his employment of traditional storytelling techniques and that most readers leave his short stories, for example, yearning for more of them, it is unfortunate that they are not in greater abundance.

CONCLUSION

Since the publication of *Things Fall Apart*, African literature, and with it Achebe's art, has made great advances, but it is unfortunate that Western interest in African literature does not advance much beyond the founding text of African literature. As acknowledged in this study, Western readers have remained charmed by *Things Fall Apart*, mostly because they can claim it as their own; but it is not enough for African nationalists to see Achebe simply as an opponent of Conrad, Greene, and other European novelists of Africa. His works must be read with full awareness of the historical authenticity within the context of colonial authorship. Achebe's use of satire and tragedy must be reconsidered. My aim in this study, then, has been to throw light on a vexing issue in the reception and interpretation of African literature: the irony that it is because of Achebe, more than any of our other writers, that African literature has enjoyed the small popularity it has in the world—and for that, we ought to be grateful to him, although that very acceptance, nay, the canonization by the West, of his first novel, should alert us to the hidden agendas of the politics of canon formation.

It is not only that the celebration of *Things Fall Apart* has been at the expense of Achebe's other works (some of which are not only more historically accurate but of greater artistic density). What is wrong is, ultimately, that *Things Fall Apart* makes a reverse perpetuation of some of the very Eurocentric assumptions it may have set out to combat, a matter that calls for a full-scale investigation.

We observe in Africa that our most profoundly enthralling and far-reaching artistic works are those which push new frontiers. They are the result of the search by their authors to extend the traditional boundaries of the genres inherited from English/French ancestry by infusing them with oral paradigms. Experimentation is thus a key determinant of quality. Indeed, as many important recent studies by Balogun[1], Julien[2], Okpewho[3], and Richards[4] have shown, readers are excited by writers like Ba[5], Osofisan[6], Sembene[7], and Ngugi,[8] mainly because of their high level of daring, for in their efforts to push the old limits of fiction, these writers turn to art forms other than the familiar, using the mode of composition that is now known as intertextual echoing.

Adaptation in the novel or drama, as each argues, reaches its turning point when the writer reconstitutes both the artistic resources and the old ideology of his/her native oral tradition as well as the novel or drama borrowed from English or French heritage, thus uniting the indigeneous and imported traditions. Similarly, our concern in this study has been to measure the level of Achebe's adventurousness, for the issue at stake is not merely the use of imported European languages or forms. On the contrary, even more important is how he uses his borrowed material. Different grades of success establish different qualities of imaginative response, measured by the ability or inability to go beyond mere imitation. *Things Fall Apart* is not only slavishly imitative of Aristotelian tragedy, it relies heavily on the conventions of the anthropology associated with the colonial novel of Africa. Achebe's reverse anthropology is wrong, because it accepts European views that present the Igbo as savages, but then proceeds apace to show that the Igbos, nevertheless, do have some form of logic, culture, law, and religion. One is relieved to find that *Arrow of God* is superior. Its contribution lies in the innovative strategies it brings to an insightful exploration of the complex factors involved in the colonial conquest of sub-Saharan Africa. The emotion evoked in *No Longer at Ease*, a transitional work, contains qualities that attempt to give shape to the character of hurt carried over from the past into contemporary society. Though it remains a novel weighted with corruption and an inability to cast off the obfuscations to reveal the hidden truth, *No Longer at Ease* is a piece whose enormous significance is only slightly reduced by its obsession with surface realism.

On a similar note, if *A Man of the People* is largely unconvincing, it is because it fails the test of artistic enactment as judged by the rquirement of visionary projection, i.e., the expectation that the committed writer display the ability not only to mass the conditions of human beings and behavior into a recognizable pattern but also to project a higher ideal. Within this context, *Anthills of the Savan-*

nah is notable. Somewhat of an ideological breakthrough, in it, the attempt to hold a mirror to the contemporary condition of the Nigeria of the 1980s is especially compelling, largely because it unveils a positive glimpse of a vision of society's redemptive values.

Mounting a new literature of post-independence self-analysis, *Anthills of the Savannah* abandons the paths of Achebe's preceding works, dealing with problems of nationhood with an emphasis that shifts from sanguine bitterness to a deeper understanding of the collective predicament of international neocolonial strangulation. Since the narrative stretches to an expanded and broader framework of class anaysis, it can be seen that some progress has been recorded in Achebe's ouevre justifying a shift from the excessive absorption with his earliest works of fiction.

It is, of course, not only an index of its quality, but also a measure of the intellectual climate of our time that many reputations have been built upon the plethora of praise endlessly poured on *Things Fall Apart* within the pages of academic journals and books across the globe. That *Things Fall Apart* has turned out to be one of those monumental works whose enormous influence can become exceedingly oppressive as to possess the capacity to stifle the critical imagination of readers worldwide is a matter to which I have attempted to call attention, for even in conclusion of this study, I am certain that I will continue to return to it in the classroom. This is the reason I urge scholars to consider the main argument that I am putting forward for consideration. Throughout the ages the struggle to unsettle established ideas has never been easy and it would simply be naive of me to expect things to change suddenly just because I am involved at this point in history.

NOTES

INTRODUCTION

1. The British leftist scholar Terry Eagleton takes us to the heart of the matter, and thereby hints at the fundamental assumptions of this study, when he encourages readers to look in each work for what he calls "sub-texts....a text which runs within it, visible at certain 'symptomatic' points of ambiguity, evasion or overemphasis, and which we as readers are able to 'write' even if the novel itself does not. All literary works contain one or more of such sub-texts, and there is a sense in which they may be spoken of as the 'unconscious' of the work itself. The work's insights, as with all writing, are deeply related to its blindness: what it does not say, how it does not say it, may be as important as what it articulates; what seems absent, marginal or ambivalent about it may provide a central clue to its meaning" *Literary Theory*, 178). The sign is critical to our conceptual grasp of literature and literary study, for sensitivity to both explicit and nonexplicit communication cues allows us to understand literature more deeply and can thus refine our appreciation of particular literary works. A text's blind spots, omissions, and gaps can be just as revealing as its explicit parts.

2. Among these works, the following must be singled out: David Carroll's sublime *Chinua Achebe* (1970), Eustace Palmer's two exellent books *An Intoduction to the African Novel* (1972) and *The Growth of the African Novel* (1979), Emmanuel Obiechina's commanding *Culture, Tradition, and Society in the West African Novel* (1975), Wole Soyinka's consummate *Myth, Literature and the African World* (1976), Kolawole Ogungbesan's concise *New West African Literature* (1979), Abiola Irele's definitive *The African Experience in Literature and Ideology* (1981), Isidore Okpewho's brilliant *Myth in Africa* (1983), Richard Bjornson's magisterial *An African Quest for Freedom* (1991), Odun Balogun's resplendent *Tradition and Modernity* (1991), Kenneth Harrow's accomplished *Thresholds of Change* (1994), Irene d'Almeida's authoritative *Francophone African Women Writers* (1994), and Chikwenye Ogunyemi's comprehensive *Africa Wo/Man Palava* (1996).

3. One elegant book appeared after my manuscript was completed and from which it would have profited: Chidi Okonkwo's *Decolonization Agnostics in Postcolonial Fiction* (1999).

CHAPTER 1

1. The slow pace of interest which we are witnessing today in the discipline of literary criticism in connection with the reconstruction of the colonial encounter is quite analogous to the same problem that afflicted the sudy of African history in the 1960s. Recall, for example, the lament of the eminent historian Basil Davidson in reference to this period, "We can say that for the time being the studying of the question of the struggle of African people is still in embryo. As a matter of fact historians have not really raised yet the problems of Africans' resistance to colonialism. It is to be supposed that many rebellions are not yet known; that historians have not yet discovered them. . . . It is not discovered yet what were the motive forces of rebellion, how they were organized, why rebels undertook one or another action, what was the inner communication between different events linked with a rebellion. About other forms of resistance we know even less than about armed rebellion" ("African Resistance and Rebellion" 177-188). Among African writers Ngugi, Sembene, Soyinka, and Armah are others who have given approximate attention to the topic of colonization and the African resistance. Critics have paid little attention to those aspects of the works of all five writers; that we still await a detailed study of colonial resistance in Africa to rival the scale and depth accomplished by James Scott in *Weapons of the Weak* about peasant revolts in south east Asia (Malaysia in particular) attests to the severity of the neglect which this important subject has suffered not only in African literary study but in African studies in general. Nonetheless, nowhere is this poverty of research more evident than in the field of African literary studies. One, therefore, looks forward with great anticipation to the arrival of works that will do for literary scholarship in relation to the depiction of colonization what works like Keletso Atkins's *The Moon Is Dead*, John Hargreaves' *West Africa Partitioned*, and Paul Stuart Landau's *The Realm of the Word*, as well as Jean and John Comaroff's two-volume study *Of Revelation and Revolution*, Jean Comaroff's *Body of Power, Spirit of Resistance*, and V. Y. Mudimbe's *Tales of Faith* have done for the respective disciplines of history and anthropology.

2. Nicholas Thomas, defining colonialism broadly as comprising what he calls "a great variety of asymmetrical inter-social relationships," makes the claim that "'colonialism' seems to have been present through most of world history in one form or another" (*Colonialism's Culture*, 3). Distinction must be made, nevertheless, between such generalized ideas and my more specific use of the term to refer to the conquest and domi-

nation of Africa by Europe, the Arab world, and America, beginning from the last turn of the nineteenth century. This point needs emphasis because even though imperial aspirations may be traced way back to an era long before the slave trade began, they were not given formal authority till the Berlin conference of 1884, when the proposal to "partition" Africa among the various European nations received the decisive official stamp of approval of the participating European nations.

3. I find my thesis corroborated in a recently published book by Belinda Edmondson, *Making Men: Gender, Literary Authority, and Women's Writing in Caribbean Narrative*, who notes the irony of male Caribbean writers such as C. L. R. James, V. S. Naipul, George Lamming, and Derek Walcot's having to "find it necessary to refract the lens of their Caribbean identity through the prism of the canonical figures of Victorian England" (1-2). This practice, Edmondson suggests, "points to a structural issue of Caribbean national identity that reaches beyond the mere espousal of ideological positions. Englishness—Victorian Englishness, no less—is somehow important in the definition of what it means to be Caribbean" (2). Of the several books that have been devoted entirely to Achebe's fiction, two are of particular relevance to the present inquiry—those by Robert Wren and Simon Gikandi. Robert Wren's *Achebe's World* is particularly important, for it offers the most detailed information that we have to date on the historical and anthropological sources upon which Achebe has drawn for his fiction. However, unlike Wren, my interest is not primarily to show proof that Achebe did make use of historical and anthropological materials (thanks to the efforts of critics like Wren, it has become possible for me now to take that to be too obvious to need corroborating), but to evaluate his uses of these within the conventional modes of fictional representation. My interpretation also breaks with Simon Gikandi's in *Reading Chinua Achebe*, in which Achebe's liberal political views completely seduce the critic into compromising the chance to offer a rigorous critique of the actual use made of historical and anthropological documents in the texts. Thus, where Gikandi stops only at deferential appreciation while reading Achebe's fiction, which he views primarily in relation to the presumed debts to European sources, I attempt to look further to uncover Achebe's successes and limitations. It seems to me a measure of indecisiveness that Gikandi begins by vacillating between believing that Achebe's motives for writing novels are "unconscious; they are only clear after the event" and a grudging acceptance that Achebe had "a self-conscious desire to produce an African literature which will use the language of the hegemonic culture to express the desire for cultural

liberation" (25). Further, Gikandi would have it, on one hand, that Achebe wrote on impulse and, on the other, would argue: "Achebe cannot start writing until he locates himself in a strategic linguistic and ideological position in relation to something else. . . an obscurantist colonial tradition" (25). Because it is his belief that "the narration of liberation derives its power from the tradition it seeks to reject, revise, or appropriate and set in a different direction" (25), Gikandi is not only deeply convinced of the futility of reading works like Achebe's outside the Western canon but also convinced that Achebe's performance is blameless. Here is a dangerous naiveté: Gikandi requires the critic who wishes to "understand the narrative techniques which Achebe adopts in *Things Fall Apart*" (and presumably all of Achebe's fiction) to "examine the ways in which the colonial tradition represses the African character, African history, and African modes of representation," but he himself fails to follow through on his wise recommendations. As he rightly perceives, "In the discourse which is evident not only in the African romances of Cary but also the 'scientific' reports of government anthropologists— Africa is represented as what David Carrol aptly calls 'a landscape without figures, an Africa without Africans'. The African has no character because he or she exists solely as a projection of European desire. . .." (27). The fix is that, because Gikandi takes Achebe's difference from his predecessors to be axiomatic—when in fact it is not— he is led to the wrong conclusion, i.e., that an alternative perspective, which is nothing short of "revolutionary," has been provided by Achebe (27). If, as I suggest, on the contrary, we take submissiveness to be forced, we can easily see why the idea is erroneous that it is more natural for subjugated peoples to assimilate and peddle rather than resist the distorted ideas that other people have about them. Nor, in my view, is the question whether one sees the element of resistance; rather, at issue should be the quality of opposition. Because unqualified adulation flows from the tendency of Achebe's critics to conflate his intentions with actual achievement, I suggest that we read Achebe's fiction more carefully than before.

4. The general dearth of literature on Islamic slavery relative to Western slavery is, of course, the result of what Bernard Lewis, in his valuable prelilimanry study *Race and Slavery in the Middle East*, has correctly called "the extreme sensitivity of the subject": Since the subject is almost a taboo, one that even Muslim scholars are so unwilling to explore and discuss as openly as Westerners, it becomes "difficult, and sometimes professionally hazardous, for a young scholar to turn his attention in this direction" (vi).

5. If there is one recurrent theme that can be said to have dominated the early study of African literature, it is the topic of African writers' debt to their presumed European mentors. It can be seen from the works of such pioneering critics as Gerald Moore (who as early as 1965 saw the ghost of Kafka all over the Guinean writer Camara Laye), and of course John Povey (who in 1971 discovered the influences of Eliot, Pound, and Hopkins on the Nigerian J. P Clark). Over the years, incorporation within the Euro-American literary tradition has defined approaches to African writing. With regard to Achebe scholarship, in particular, the reading of his counter texts in light of his presumed Western ancestors has been pursued like an obsession, almost as an end in itself. Thus, even as recently as 1990, Mildred Mortimer begins her study, *Journeys Through the French African Novel*, discussing Conrad's influence, which she sees in the major African writers across different geographical regions; and nearly all the contributors to the 1991 MLA-sponsored *Approaches to the Teachings of Achebe's Things Fall Apart*, edited by Bernth Lindfors, lend the position confirmation, to the extent that in Edna Aizenberg's solitary study, which places Achebe within the "Third World Literary Discourse," Achebe is compared not with a fellow African but with a Latin American writer—Guatemalan Nobel Prize winner Miguer Angel Asturias. Similarly, the goal of C. L. Innes' recent book *Chinua Achebe* is to demonstrate that Achebe's writings—though inevitably about African subjects—are yet deeply embedded, formalistically, within the Western tradition. Specifically, by showing that Joyce Cary's *Mister Johnson*, for example, is central to the form and design of "Achebe's first two novels" (12), Innes is of course merely following the well-worn paths traversed earlier by her predecessors such as Molly Mahood, A. G. Stock, Roderick Wilson, and Robert Wren. What sets my work apart from that of all these critics is that all of them have observed Achebe's use of Western writers without really scrutinizing the impact of those sources on the overall picture that emerges from his writing; this the gap that my study seeks to fill.

6. In his magisterial study, *Mimesis: The Representation of Reality in Western Literature* (1946), Eric Auerbach lends powerful affirmation to the issue of representation's intricacy. All his astute readings imply that it is necessary that the aspiring creator be not only exceptionally attentive to his/her surroundings, circumstances, events, and objects to attain a visual presence; in addition, it is necessary that the aspiring creative author be exceptionally gifted with powers of verbal or visual expression to carry it through successfully. Auerbach maintains that background may not be everything, but it is deeply embed-

ded in the work of art. Background is acutely relevant to the business of interpretation, because every writer is directly or indirectly the product of his/her environment. It is in this connotation I developed the concept of the politics of representation in this book.

7. Karin Barber states this conventional view beautifully in her cogent study *I Could Speak Until Tomorrow* (1991), where she reminds us that it is not always wise to rely on authorial intentions because "[t]he text itself says more than it knows; it generates 'surplus': meanings that go beyond, and may subvert, the purported intention of the work. It has the capacity to pick up subterranean ideological impulses that are brought to realization in no other discursive arena" (3).

8. See Mahmood Mamdani's magisterial work *Citizen and Subject* for more on this subject.

9. See, for example, Ngugi's *A Grain of Wheat*. What makes a historical work like Ngugi's so dazzling is the major statement it makes about the place of revision in the African creative practice. Through its dialogue with *Things Fall Apart* and then its sequel *Arrow of God*, *A Grain of Wheat* makes a major contribution to African literature. In it, Ngugi deploys his borrowed materials with great imagination, and he emerges as an innovative writer whose individuality lies in the way he skillfully brings the elements of many great narrative traditions into fresh combinations: history and myth as well as orality and writing. While managing overall to identify with the primary objectives of his Nigerian counterpart to use the novel for furthering liberation efforts, Ngugi at the same time, turns down any pretension to the sort of anthropological descriptivess that has been found to be objectionable in Achebe. Because Ngugi does not aspire to the same level of vividness one finds in accounts of African tribal life that Achebe provides in his fiction, Ngugi does not expose himself to the same insidious allegations to which Achebe is so often subjected: for example, the claim that Achebe is a reverse colonialist writer or one who participates in the curious act of justifying the existence of his people to foreigners.

10. Arlene Elder, "The Paradoxical Characterization," in Lindfors, ed., *Approaches to the Teaching of Achebe's Things Fall Apart*, p.55.

11. A. D. Nuttall, *Why Does Tragedy Give Pleasure?* pp.83-84.

12. Although many younger African writers also tap from the oral tradition, their nearly total avoidance of proverbial expression habitual with Achebe suggests that younger writers harbor deep suspicions about its relevance to the vision of the world they wish to propose. On this most crucial device in Achebe's fiction, at least one critic, Chantal Zabus in her book *The African Palimpsest*, contends that

though it may serve as Achebe's most vital link with the oral tradition, when extrapolated from its original context and placed in written texts, such as Achebe's novels, the proverb inevitably experiences a form of "disability," because writing itself is "closely associated with death." As she explains further, by reducing proverbs to writing, Achebe cuts them from their "original context" and they "fall prey to a textual glottophagia whereby the Igbo proverbs are 'eaten' by the English words of the European narrative" (145-6). Moreover, Zabus equates the whole exercise to "a treason," a cultural mutation reminiscent of "the treacherous kiss" that "signalled the beginning of echoic recitation between the talmid and the Rabbi...turned into a Judas kiss" (146).

13. For an extended treatment of this topic, especially of francophone texts, see Mildred Mortimer's *Journeys Through the French African Novel*. Another interesting discussion is contained in Janos Reisz's "Mariam Ba's *Une si longue lettre.*"

14. Achebe's attacks on *The Beautyful Ones Are Not Yet Born* in his "Africa and Her Writers" (*Morning Yet on Creation Day Essays*, 19-29), may indicate otherwise, but the revealing fact is that his claims on committed literature are not always in harmony with his own artistic performance. Achebe must have made those remarks because he felt his own practice was more socially committed, and therefore more political, than Armah's, but a careful investigation reveals that he is simply nursing a pipe-dream whose total lack of merit is too self-evident to need remarking. As if to confirm the adage, "what goes around, comes around," Wole Soyinka has made similar comments on one of Achebe's own novels, in his *Myth, Literature, and the African World*, 87-8, 90-95; Buabeki Jabbi responds to these strictures in his vigorous essay "Myth and Ritual in *Arrow of God.*"

15. Simon Gikandi, for example, admires its "concern with the power and authority of storytelling, of the function of the storyteller in the contemporary African situation, and the relationship of writers and intellectuals to the men of power in the postcolonial state" (*Reading Achebe* 125). Elleke Boehmer quotes with obvious approval Ben Okri's review, which casts the novel as Achebe's "most complex and his wisest book to date" ("of Goddesses and Stories"). According to Emmanuel Ngara, "Character portrayal and the use of language alone do not fully account for the success of Achebe's art. There is, in addition, the writer's skill in telling the story, his narrative technique," and in *Anthills*, Ngara believes, Achebe has "risen to new heights in both artistic excellence and social vision" ("Achebe as Artist," in Rutherford and Petersen, ed. *Chinua Achebe: A Celebration* 113). In

the rather eulogistic issue of the journal *Matatu* devoted entirely to the novel, editor Holger G. Ehling describes the book as being "the most important novel to come out of Africa in the eighties," a work that, he adds, "comprises the sum total of Achebe's political and literary thinking as well as his attempt to come to terms with Nigerian politics and society; here we find new modes of thought, new patterns of discourse" (*Critical Approaches to Anthills* 1). Unfortunately none of the six selected essays attempts to locate the place of the novel within the whole corpus of the African novels written in the decade of its publication. Instead, all focus on the novel's polemical thrust; but only two of the critics (David Maughan-Brown and Patricia Alden) even venture into evaluative criticism of the book's political and aesthetic significance. In *"Anthills of the Savannah*: Achebe's Solution to the *Trouble with Nigeria*,*"* in Ehling, ed. *Critical Approaches to Anthills*, Maughan-Brown explores how the novel "sets out to solve a problem, and makes large claims for the authority of story-tellers in so doing" (6). After subjecting the novel to the general "Third World, political debate" and extensively considering "the context of the message; and the way in which the action of the plot is made to demonstrate the essential points of the author's thesis" (7), Maughan-Brown finds the work seriously flawed. Maughan Brown certaily over-states the case somewhat, and the need to strike a balance between these two extremist positions cannot be ignored, for the truth lies somewhere in the middle.

CHAPTER 2

1. V. Y. Mudimbe, *The Invention of Africa*, p.1.
2. When, in his *Parables & Fables*, Mudimbe elaborates on his astonishing claims about the operation of colonialism's structure, it is not really clear if he is being merely sarcastic or hypothetical, or means to be understood as stating a historical/factual/literal reality. These are his words, however: "The Surface of emergence of Western colonial responsibility explains and makes necessary colonization as a global activity for converting a non-Western space into a Western-marked area." He adds: "The inscription of Western Christianity and its African incarnation grounds the power and the meaning of these systems and the explanatory effects of political actions. Thus, a missionary arrives in an African village. He or she meets the local chief, amicably negotiates a sojourn, and, in most cases, is accepted without problem. The event immediately degenerates into a pattern repeated throughout the continent. The missionary first establishes in the vil-

lage a network of friends and sympathizers by recourse to generous initiatives and gifts. Second, he or she makes familiar his or her presence by associating it directly with the effeciency of a serving..." (7). Mudimbe's story is of course contradicted by the greater majority of those told by such historians of the colonial occupation and rule in Africa as Anene, Boahen, Isichei, Hargreaves, and Afigbo. One need only compare his ideas with the picture of the resistance that other African peoples, including the Igede (one of the Igbo's immediate northern neighbors) offer of the colonial occupation. Ogede documents this case in his *Art, Society, and Performance* 2-4. See also Chapter One of Jean and John Comaroff's monumental study *Of Revelation and Revolution*, about a similar response by the Tswana of southern Africa, as well as Paul Landau's *The Realm of the Word*, which provides similar explorationss of other resistant southern African groups. Even though the period of European conquest and occupation has been described, notably by Professor Adu Boahen, as "the most bloody and the most brutal of all the stages of the Scramble from the Afrocentric standpoint" (*African Perspectives* 34), it must never be forgotten that we still live with the consequences of colonization. Because colonization created psychological effects that are no less traumatic than the physical assaults of conquest, as they have involved the diversion of African peoples from their normal state of being, its lingering effects—mental, psychological, cultural, etc.—must be accorded recognition equal to that given to the physical violence that attended it.

3.   See Chinua Achebe, "African Literature," p.7. Achebe alters this view slightly in his new book *Home and Exile*, stressing that it was the misrepresentation of Africa in works of English writers that provoked him to write a rebuttal. One episode Achebe couldn't forget occurred in his class at the University College, Ibadan: During the early 1950s, one of his classmates "stood up and told an astounded teacher point-blank that the moment he had enjoyed" in Joyce Cary's *Mister Johnson*, a book usually seen by Europeans as "the best novel ever written about Africa," was when "the Nigerian hero, Johnson, was shot to death by his British master, Mr. Rudbeck." He adds: "The rest of us, now astounded too, offered a medley of noises in reaction.... we all shared our colleague's exasperation at this bumbling idiot of a character whom Joyce Cary and our teacher were so assiduously passing off as a poet when he was nothing but an embarrassing nitwit! Now, this incident, as I came to recognize later, was more than just an interesting episode in a colonial classroom. It was a landmark rebellion. Here was a whole class of young Nigerian students, among the brightest of their generation, united in their view of a book of English

fiction in complete opposition to their English teacher, who was more-over backed by the authority of metropolitan critical judgment" (22-23).

4. Chinua Achebe, *Things Fall Apart*, p.3.

5. Chinua Achebe, Ibid. pp. 97-98.

6. Ibid. p. 99.

7. Ibid. p. 99

8. Though Wren discusses these matters as background material, as supplemental information needed for understanding Achebe's nov-els, he never really considers limiting their abridgement in the novels; on the contrary, Wren sees the accomplishment of *Things Fall Apart* as depending more on its omissions than on its inclusions, for it is his belief that all great novels have what he calls "something of the com-pression of poetry, which says much in little" (*Achebe's World* 9). Needless to say, the limitation of such a perspective is that it leaves out such world masterpieces as Balzac's *Madame Bovary*, Defoe's *Moll Flanders*, Joyce's *Ulysses*, to say nothing of Melville's *Moby Dick* and even Achebe's own later novel, *Arrow of God*, all of which derive strengths from striving for inclusiveness, for a comprehen-siveness of detail, for an expansiveness in coverage.

9. See Elizabeth Isichei, *The Igbo and the Europeans*, 109ff. Because among the Igbos both humans and their gods place primacy on the sanctity of human life, the story of the slaughters accompanying the colonial wars should have been pivotal in a text like Achebe's for its claims to historical authenticity to be validated. Hunt Hawkins main-tains that Achebe reverses the European charges of savagery against Africa by showing that the "wars among the Igbos are relatively minor, ritualized affairs, while the Europeans create real violence. In local wars, for instance, Okonkwo brings home only five heads, but the Europeans wipe out the village of Abame" ("*Things Fall Apart* and the Literature of Empire" 81). However, I believe Achebe could have made the contrast sharper. He suggests colonial violence, but never fully develops it in his text. Readers must distinguish between Achebe's intention and his accomplishments. To read meaning for which textual evidence is lacking is to commit an intentional fallacy. Since this issue borders on the mishandling of the notion of determi-nate meaning, Hawkins's imputations are misleading.

10. See Elizabeth Isichei, *A History of the Igbo People*, p. 119.

11. Achebe, "African Literature," in Rutherford and Petersen, ed. *Chinua Achebe: A Celebration*, p. 7.

12. Several of the statements that Naipul made in that interview now prove prophetic. For example, he had pointed out that European tastes, European capital, and European audiences would continue to set the

criteria for successful art in most of Africa until conditions improved for writers in Africa. Naipul's warning that Africa would continue to lose most of her intelligentsia, forced to emigrate to other lands in search of greener pastures is now a painful reality. Africans themselves have not heeded the call he had made for a return to the vernacular in education, politics, and in business, which alone, Naipul believed, could restore confidence in the use of indigeneous languages in literary expression, in turn freeing African writers from dependence on European values and European publishers. See his interview with Adrian Rowe-Evans.

13. See Barbara Harlow, *Resistance Literature*, p. 7.

14. Chidi Amuta states the case cogently in his essay "Literature of the Nigerian Civil War": "To be familiar with Nigerian Literature in the period between 1970 and the present is to be conversant with one dominant and recurrent area of social concern: the Nigerian Civil War (1967-70) .... And given the statistical dominance of Nigerian Literary works in African Literature, the Nigerian Civil War could well be said to be the single most imaginatively recreated historical experience in Africa so far" (85). Achebe did disclose, in an interview with Nwachukwu-Agbada before the 1987 publication of *Anthills of the Savannah*, that he was planning to turn to the civil war—an indirect admission that he himself is not happy with this state of affairs, for the gap left in Nigerian literary history by the dearth of material on the civil war is a major one. Needless to say, when Achebe does finally come around to initiating such a project, it will represent not only a much-needed expansion of his own range, but a great advance for Nigerian fiction as a whole (see "A Conversation with Chinua Achebe," 122, for details on this).

15. See details in Chinua Achebe's essay "An Image of Africa: Racism in Conrad's *Heart of Darkness*," in Harper and Stepto, ed. *Chant of Saints*, 313-25.

16. Ibid. p. 321.

17. See Nwachukwu-Agbada, "A Conversation with Chinua Achebe," in *Commonwealth: Essays and Studies* 13.1 (1990): 117-24.

18. Rhonda Cobham, in her article "Making Men and History: Achebe and the Politics of Revision," points out other central ideas explored in *Things Fall Apart* that she believes are essentially Western in orientation, arguing that "although the novel tells us of Okonkwo's many wives and children, the male-female relationships in Okonkwo's family that Achebe isolates for our scrutiny are almost indistinguishable from those of monogamous couples in Western tradition" (96). Pressing her point, she goes on to say that she "never really see[s]

Okonkwo's wives interacting with one another the way we see the men interacting among themselves or even Okonkwo interacting with his children. From a Western perspective the omission is hardly experienced as a loss . . . . its similarity to Western versions of marriage may help explain why students spontaneously empathize with Ekwefi when Okonkwo mistreats her and why they often read the text as misogynist" (96). While I do not doubt the convergence of certain Western and African notions of life in *Things Fall Apart*, from some of Cobham's statements about Okonkwo's wives, it is clear that she missed both scenes of communal cooking, where Okonkwo's wives are presented as they prepare for the celebration of the New Yam Festival (Chapter Five, pages 26-32) and to mark the thanksgiving ceremony that Okonkwo orgainizes for his mother's kinsmen toward the end of his days in exile (Chapter Nineteen, pages 115-118). Another occasion where women come together in the novel in a manner that suggests only polygamous circumstances occurs in Chapter Twelve, during the bride-offering ceremony. Unquestionably the best picture of the Igbo communal values is that presented toward the end of the novel, when Okonkwo asks his three wives to get "things together for a great feast," so that he can thank his mother's people for having taken care of him during his period of exile; in that scene, we sense the kernel of the women's work ethic—the sharing, delegation of duty, and sisterhood without rancor:

> Ekwefi still had some cassava left on her farm from the previous year. Neither of the other wives had. It was not that they had been lazy, but that they had many children to feed. It was therefore understood that Ekwefi would provide cassava for the feast. Nwoye's mother and Ojiugo would provide the other things like smoked fish, palm oil and pepper for the soup. Okonkwo would Take care of meat and yams. (117)

From the above passage it can be seen that everything falls into place when roles are accepted with humor by everyone in the family. There is a sense of the social harmony that follows naturally when members of a community accept their social responsibilities: the feast begins with the convocation of "all the descendants of Okolo, who had lived about two hundred years before" (117). In the prayer that Uchendu, "the oldest member of this extensive family," says summarizing the underlying philosophy that guides the life of the people:

> The kola nut was given to him to break, and he prayed to the ancestors. He asked them for health and children.'We

do not ask for wealth because he that has health and children will also have wealth. We do not pray to have more
money but more kinsmen. We are better than animals because we have kinsmen. An animal rubs its aching flank
against a tree, a man asks his kinsman to scratch him.' He
prayed especially for Okonkwo and his family. He then broke
the Kola nut and threw one of the lobes on the ground for
the ancestors.(117)

Achebe takes care to explain that the food (pottage, foofoo, and
especially the meat) is shared in such a way so that "every member of
the *umunna* had a portion"(117-8). In sharing the meat, for instance,
physical presence is not a factor. "Every man rose in order of years
and took a share. Even the kinsmen who had not been able to come
had their shares taken out for them in due turn" (118). Here we sense
the generosity, the honest intimacy, and the involved interest the
people take in each other's lives. The communal ethic banishes greed
and selfishness entirely from the community, and the people eschew
an unnecessary show of power and influence as well as any pretense
of friendship.

Appropriately, Achebe's most telling statement about the fundamental principles behind the African cultural community is conveyed
by "one of the oldest members of the umunna" (118). He is even older
than Okonkwo's uncle Uchendu, we might surmise. That he remains
deliberately anonymous makes him stand out all the more creditably
as the voice of traditional wisdom. During his closing remarks at the
party, he thanks Okonkwo for giving them such a lavish feast. However,
he goes further, using the occasion to impress upon everyone present
that the governing ideals of the community are the sharing, the joy that
comes from sharing, and the opportunity people have to show sincere
love for one another. It is the love of humanity, and our common
knowledge of our identity that is best celebrated cooperatively.

'...It is good in these days when the younger generation
consider themselves wiser than their sires to see a man
doing things in the grand old way. A man who calls his
kinsmen to a feast does not do so to save them from starv-
ing. They all have food in their own home.
When we gather together in the moonlit village ground it
is not because of the moon. Every man can see it in his own
compound. We come together because it is good for kinsmen to do so. You may ask why I am saying all this. I say it
because I fear for the younger generation, for you people.'

> He waved his arm where most of the young men sat, 'As for me, I have only a short while to live, and so have Uchendu and Unachukwu and Emefo. But I fear for you young people because you do not understand how strong is the bond of kinship. You do not know how to speak with one voice. And what is the result? An abominable religion has settled among you .... (118)

The old man's words prove prophetic: At the end of the novel, Okonkwo kills the British District Commissioner's messenger in defense of tradition, he doesn't get the support of his kinsmen. Devastated by the lack of unity among his people, Okonkwo goes to hang himself. The British assumed control, and Achebe uses Okonkwo's suicide as an effective means to suggest that the absence of unity among Africans is responsible for their defeat.

In his next novel, *Arrow of God*, Achebe presents women more in their public roles: two male contestants, Ezeulu and Nwaka employ the women in their lives in the personal rivalry.

19. See Florence Stratton, *African Literature and Gender*, p. 22.
20. Benedict Anderson, *Imagined Communities*.
21. Ibid. pp. 141-42.
22. Achebe, *Things Fall Apart*, pp. 133-34.
23. Kofi Owusu, "The Politics of Interpretation," p. 460.
24. For more on the "comic" Irish figure, see Daniel Corkey's *Synge and Anglo-Irish Literature*.
25. Robert Wren attempted to raise and address these kinds of questions, when he asked, "What did Umofia buy with the new money that flowed into the town?" Wren's answer, as should be expected, is: "Nothing, it must be said, of much value, nor anything really new. Aro traders had brought cotton cloth, tobacco, beads, and gin to those who could afford them throughout the nineteenth century. Umofia bought a little cloth, a few beads, and some tobacco for snuff before the white man came, and at least talked about gin. Now these came in abundance, and porcelain plates and iron as well. Such trade may not have improved life in Umofia much, but to the colonial it was a move toward 'civilization'" (*Achebe's World*, 30). How curious that Achebe should worship such trifles!
26. See Gananath Obeyesekere, *The Apotheosis of Captain Cook*, p.3.
27. Achebe, *Things Fall Apart*, p. 130.
28. Ibid. p. 126.
29. Romanus Muoneke brings together all the kinds of misconceptions held about the work of European missionaries in Africa by stating in his study *Art, Rebellion and Redemption*: "The missionaries, them-

selves, included people who exhibited exemplary qualities. An example is Mr. Brown who displayed the vitality of Christain faith in his reverence for his fellow man. He educated the people and cared for their welfare. His willingness to listen to the people and learn from them about their own culture enabled him to carry out his mission in a very hospitable manner. He not only cared for the people's spiritual welfare by building new churches, he also cared for their material progress; hence, he built a school and a hospital" (110-11). Such an argument misses the distinction between, on one hand, what colonization did to the few Africans it forced to assimilate the cultural model of the conqueror, the few Africans elevated from the margins of society; and, on the other, what colonization did to the majority of the population whose culture was destroyed in the process, for colonization was basically a system of injustice that, by reversing positions, placed the minority group formerly in the margin at the top. It is evident that Muoneke is not addressing the question from the position of that larger population whose situation ought to be more critical, since the survival of the group as a whole is more important than that of its parts; instead, he is viewing the question from the position of those formerly on the periphery, the minority population that has been favored. Nor should the issue be whether Brown successfully carried out his mandate to help the formerly disadvantaged group; since Brown's mission as a missionary is not to preserve but to undermine the culture of the conquered people, Munuoneke's attribution of what he calls "the growth" of the new faith to the suppossed goodness of such individuals as Brown misses the main issue: the massive destruction colonization waged against the culture of the indigeneous people, whose lives were diverted from their natural states. Had Muoneke taken a moment to reflect on the nature of colonization, he might have seen it clearly for what is was—a meddling affair that caused much suffering for its victims; he might also have realized that, for the victims, therefore, the motives for colonization, i.e., the excuses that the imperialists used for venturing out, the reasons they claimed drove them out to colonize, are immaterial, since their determination of what the Africans' needs were was based upon outside assumptions, a criteria established not by Africans themselves but by the snoopers who, having unfairly compaired the African societies they met with their own societies at home, were attempting to make Africans replicas of Europeans.

30. For details of Achebe's debts to European writers, see the studies by David Carroll, Eustace Palmer, and Ben Obumselu. It seems to me that Simon Gikandi's attempt to read *Things Fall Apart* with

poststructuralist tools is not so successful however. Following Carroll specifically, Gikandi describes Achebe's first novel as "a heterodiegetic narrative—one in which the narrator is not a character in the narrated situations or events." However, he is not so persuasive when he warns that "our concern should not be with the personality of this narrator, nor his/her identity; rather our emphasis should be on how this narrator functions in the text and on how his/her shifting focalization, the different perspectives 'in terms of which the narrated situations and events are presented'" (*Reading Chinua Achebe* 45). I personally doubt the wisdom of such an approach and suggest that the reader who wants to gain a proper grasp of this text not disregard the identity of the narrator, because it is crucial to any attempt to offer an adequate assessment of the function he performs in the text, as indeed support for consideration of the identity of the narrator in such a light was long ago provided by Robert Scholes and Robert Kellogg, who argue strongly in their authoritative book *The Nature of Narrative* (especially in relation to the eye-witness narrator) that "considerations of character are intimately related to considerations of point of view" (256). In order to determine the reliability of any narrator, the question of character will always be paramount; the heterodiegetic narrative in *Things Fall Apart* cannot be an exception.

31. See Oladele Taiwo, *Culture in the Nigerian Novel*, p. 123.
32. Achebe, *Things Fall Apart*, p. 111.
33. Chinua Achebe, *Things Fall Apart*, p. 111.
34. See Chinua Achebe, *No Longer at Ease*.
35. Gareth Griffiths, "Language and Action," p. 68.
36. I do not dispute the fact that the novel evokes some level of emotion, for the figure of Okonkwo and his tragic fate, the idea of an inflexible and stubborn but passionate individual, caught up in circumstances he can hardly comprehend, is quite painful in itself. So, without question, is the last duty Obierika performs for his friend, covering for the cultural hero before the British District Commissioner: clearly one of the most moving events in literature, one which demonstrates tolerance, courage, and calm reasoning in a moment of severe stress, one in which we see a kind-hearted and generous man extending to a fellow human being qualities this same individual so tragically lacked in his own life. Nonetheless, moving as these episodes are, the use of hero Okonkwo's death to end the novel raises questions concerning how we respond to a work where a writer takes the easy way out to resolve what is unarguably a complex and unsolvable problem. The inappropriateness of this technique, it would seem, lies in the fact that the novel personalizes what is clearly a historical movement, in

the event, reducing to the personal level a problem that transcends the individual.

37. Though C. L. Innes in "A Source for *Arrow of God*—A Response" offers a hot challenge to Nnolim's claims, few would doubt that more intense foray into Igbo history has brought much gains for Achebe's art in *Arrow of God*. Thus, even though all of Nnolim's claims might not have been fully substantiated, he does point to issues that critics would explore with profit. Innes' argument that "Achebe based his novel on an actual incident, recorded by Simon Nnolim in *The History of Umuchu*, in which a priest called Ezeagu rejected a chieftaincy in 1913, was imprisoned and refused to roast the sacred yams for the months missed" and her claim that "*Arrow of God* can be seen as yet another response by Achebe to *Mister Johnson* and the literary and historical perspective it represents" (*Chinua Achebe* 64) appear to be contradictory.

38. Achebe, *Arrow of God*, p. 20.

39. Ibid. p. 37.

40. Ibid. pp.37-38.

41. See David Carroll, *Chinua Achebe*, p. 99.

42. In his book *Stylistic Criticism and the African Novel*, Emmanuel Ngara describes the structure of Nwaka's speech as observing the following pattern: a formal opening, followed by expansive commentary, and a conclusion (see especially pages 62-3). What Ngara omits, however, are the para-linguistic devices of orality such as body movement, which Nwaka utilizes to get the audience on his side. Atmosphere is very crucial to Nwaka's effects, for, like the traditional bard, he creates real rapport with his audience. This is evident when Nwaka begins by speaking "almost softly"; but, as soon as they begin to sound "murmurs of approval and disapproval but more of approval," Nwaka "walked forward and back as he spoke" evidently exploiting the manner in which "the eagle feather in his red cap and bronze band on his ankle marked him out as one of the lords of the land—a man favoured by *Eru*, the god of riches" (*Arrow of God*, 16).

43. For an alternative to the reading that I am proposing, see Adeleke Adeeko's article "Contest of Text and Context" and Neil ten Kortenaar's "Beyond Authenticity and Creolization." Both critics accuse the Akukalia-led team of botching their roles as emissaries of a peace plan, thus missing Achebe's point—that the messenger as a human agent is expected to bring to his mission some improvising, personal attitude. That Achebe is not alone in attributing the Igbo's defeat to lack of unity is worth noting. E. N. Obiechina, another Igbo man of letters, also blames the members of Igbo society for failing to forge a

united front against the invaders; for him, "Okonkwo's example suggests that traditional society did not provide complete security to the traditional individual against the irrational and inhuman forces that threatened his well-being, especially if the individual had, like Okonkwo, some overpowering personal weakness. When such an individual was struck down, he was struck down alone, but the tragic experience was lived through vicariously by the other members of the community with whom his life was linked" (*Culture, Tradition and Society* 216). We have seen, on the contrary, from the extensive historical researches of Elizabeth Isichei and the eminent Igbo historian A. E. Afigbo, that the Igbo did unite in an attempt to defend their territory. Other African writers such as Ngugi and Sembene have utilized more recent historical evidence from other parts of Africa to disprove the theory of inbred disunity of African peoples during colonization. In Ngugi's *A Grain of Wheat* and Sembene's *God's Bits of Wood*, we find detailed documentation of numerous resistance efforts in both East and West Africa, where many African peoples successfully united in their struggle against domination.

44. Achebe, *Arrow of God*, p.17.
45. Ibid. p.18.
46. Ibid. p.91.
47. Ibid. p.92.
48. Ibid. p.92.
49. Ibid. p.126.
50. Taiwo, *Culture and the Nigerian Novel*, p.138.
51. Soyinka, *Myth, Literature, and the African World*, pp.91-92.
52. For an informative discussion of this topic, see David Carroll's *Chinua Achebe*, pp.95-105.
53. Achebe, *Arrow of God*, p.132.
54. See Obiechina, "The Human Dimension," pp.177-78.
55. Achebe, *Arrow of God*, p.229.
56. Achebe, *Arrow of God*, p.228.
57. G. D. Killam, *The Writings of Chinua Achebe*, p.61.

CHAPTER 3

1. See C. L. Innes' fascinating discussion in her *Chinua Achebe*, p.8.
2. John Hollander, *The Work of Poetry*.
3. The attempt to transpose British education into the colony has forced Innes in *Chinua Achebe* (p. 8) to rethink the distinctions that people too often make between formal instruction in the metropole and that in the colony. Kole Omotoso in *Achebe and Soyinka* (p.1) adds his

voice when he describes both the educational and social experiences unique to the "only children who lived in secluded areas in the early years of the creation of the educated elite in Nigeria": the children of "teachers and employees of the Church Missionary Society or the Roman Catholic Church—clergymen, pastors and their higher officials such as headmasters and school inspectors"—who all lived a secluded life and who were thus afflicted with a seeping alienation right from a very early stage in their upbringing. In Omotoso's words, "These children saw the world from behind the hibiscus flower fences and rose gardens of the parsonage or the missionary school compound. Their lives were wrapped up in the power of the written word either through the Bible or the hymnal companion or the publications of the church as well as the teachers' manuals. They had their places of play-the fields and farms left to them after all the other children had gone home to their houses and huts in the towns and villages. Discouraged from playing any games of chance such as Ludo, Snakes and Ladders and any card games, these special children had only books to play with and they were usually competent in reading even before they began their formal education."

4. Madeleine Coltenet-Hage and Kevin Meehan, "Our Ancestors the Gauls," p.76. Janos Reisz, "*Une si Longue Lettre*: An Erziehungroman" is an excellent reading of the theme of education in the francophone African novel by Mariama Ba, *Une si Longue Lettre.*

5. Chinua Achebe, *No Longer At Ease*, London: Heinemann, 1960, p.9. All page references depend on this edition.

6. Ibid. p.6.

7. Ibid. p.28.

8. David Cook, *African Literature*, p. 84. In light of Professor Cook's cogent observation on the destructive effects of Western education, there is something disingenious about his conclusion that both from "childhood experience and adult study Obi is better placed than others to cross the dividing lines in this sectionalized society," p.93. The opposite is true, because everything in Obi's education has sought to estrange him from his culture while failing to give him a coherent alternative identity.

9. See Umelo Ojinmah's *Chinua Achebe: New Perspectives* (42-43) for an intelligent calculation of Obi's limited income relative to his overburdened expenditures. Despite his stimulating argument, the tenacity of Ayi Kwei Armah's hero—the man, who, in the face of being despised for his poverty, resists corruption to the end in *The Beautyful Ones Are Not Yet Born*—is reassurance that poverty is not a good excuse for falling into moral decline.

10. Achebe, *No Longer at Ease*, p.141.
11. Ibid. p.141.
12. Ibid. p.84.
13. Ibid. p.3. From the picture of Green's personality that Miss Tomlinson provides, the English officer who shares an office with Obi and knows their boss intimately, one senses the image of a typically paternalistic white liberal, who is very comfortable with "uneducated" Africans but spites the educated ones. It is no wonder that he pays the school fees for his steward's children and provides regular financial support for his messsenger Charles. Green, devoted to duty in the single-minded way only a liberal can be, loves the poor with the sympathy of a Catholic, and exhibits the missionary zeal of the colonialist who "must have come originally with an ideal—to bring light to the heart of darkness, the tribal head-hunters performing weird ceremonies and unspeakable rites" (96). The real situation in Africa, which contradicts the stereotype that Green wants to believe, constitutes the material for Achebe's reversal of the colonialists's myth of African primitivity.
14. See Robert Wren, *The Historical and Cultural Context*, p. 63.
15. Achebe, *No Longer at Ease*, p.40.
16. Ibid. p.5.
17. Innes, *Chinua Achebe*, p.43.
18. Achebe, *No Longer at Ease*, pp.64-65.
19. Ibid. p.52.
20. Ibid. p.53.
21. Walter Rodney, *How Europe Underdeveloped Africa*, pp. 240-241.
22. Achebe, *No Longer at Ease*, pp.7-8.
23. Ibid. p.45.
24. N. F. Inyama, "Genetic Discontinuity," p.122.
25. Achebe, *No Longer at Ease*, p.121.
26. Eustace Palmer, *An Introduction to the African Novel*, p.7o.
27. Achebe, *No Longer at Ease*, p.123.
28. Frederick Jameson, *The Political Unconscious*, p. 48.
29. Achebe, *A Man of the People*, p.4.
30. Ibid. p.7.
31. Ibid. p.2.
32. Robert Scholes and Robert Kellog, *The Nature of Narrative*, p.164.
33. Achebe, *A Man of the People*, p.12.
34. Ibid. p.15.
35. Adewale Maja-Pearce, *A Mask Dancing*, p.38.
36. Ibid. p.39.
37. Obiechina, *Culture, Tradition*, p.156.

38. Chantal Zabus, *The African Palimpsest*, p.138.
39. Daniel Corkey, *Synge and Anglo-Irish literature*, pp.7-8.
40. Gikandi, *Reading Chinua Achebe*, pp.102-103.
41. Zabus, *The African Palimpsest*, p.143.
42. Obiechina, *Culture, Tradition*, p.150.
43. Rosemary Colmer, "Quis Custodiet?" in *Chinua Achebe: A Celebration*, edited by Anna Rutherford and Kirsten Holst Petersen, p.97.
44. Bernth Lindfors, "Achebe's African Parable," *Presence Africaine* 66 (1968), p.249.
45. Ibid. p.254.
46. Ibid. p.254.
47. Eric Heyne, "Toward a Theory of Literary Nonfiction," in *Modern Fiction Studies* 33.3 (1987), p.488.
48. Emmanuel Udumukwu, "Achebe and the Negation of Independence," in *Modern Fiction Studies* 37.3 (1991), 479.
49. The autobiographical slant of *A Man of the People* has been discussed widely. See, for instance, Kole Omotoso, *Achebe and Soyinka*, and Charles Larson, *The Emergence of African Fiction*.
50. Obiechina, *Culture, Tradition*, p.150.
51. Colmer, "Quis Custodiet?" 90.
52. Biodun Jeyifo, "For Chinua Achebe," p.60.
53. Gikandi, *Reading Chinua Achebe*, p.122.
54. G. D. Killam, *The Novels of Chinua Achebe*, p.92.
55. Lindfors, "Achebe's African Parable," p.248-54.
56. Gikandi, *Reading Chinua Achebe*, pp.107-108.
57. Ibid. p.124.
58. M. J. C. Echeruo, "Chinua Achebe," pp.160-61.
59. Achebe, *A Man of the People*, p.37.
60. Ibid. p.56.
61. Gerald Moore, *Twelve African Writers*, p. 137.
62. Colmer, "Quis Custodiet?" p.100.
63. See Eustace Palmer, *An Introduction to the African Novel*, p.72. In his book *The Emergence of African Literature*, Charles Larson makes oblique reference to this central weakness of Achebe's art, writing as follows on p.153: "In many ways this novel [*A Man of the People*] is his weakest so far, and I am convinced that its popularity with the African reading audience bears little correlation to its literary merits."
64. Achebe, *Anthills of the Savannah*, p.4.
65. Ibid. p.10.
66. Gikandi, *Reading Chinua Achebe*, p.131.
67. Achebe, *Anthills of the Savannah*, p.15.
68. Ibid. p.45.

69. Ibid. p.141.
70. Ibid. p.141.
71. Ibid. p.142.
72. Ibid. p.146.
73. Patricia Alden, "New Women, Old Myths," pp.67-8.
74. Patricia Alden, "New Women, Old Myths," p.68.
75. Ibid. p.69.
76. Achebe, *Anthills of the Savannah*, p.146.
77. Ibid. p.68.
78. Ibid. p.68.
79. Ibid. p.74.
80. Alden, "New Women, Old Myths," p.72.
81. Ibid. pp.72-73.
82. Achebe, *Anthills of the Savannah*, p.67.
83. Ibid. p.102.
84. Ibid. p.80.
85. Ibid. p.58.

CHAPTER 4

1. Willfried Feuser, *Jazz and Palmwine*, p.iv.
2. My references will depend on the Heinemann edition of *Girls at War and Other Stories*, 1972.
3. See Chinua Achebe, *Home and Exile*, pp.3-16.
4. Also, see Ruth Finnegan, *Oral Literature in Africa*, and Harold Scheub, *Story*.
5. Ossie Enekwe, "Chinua Achebe's Short Stories," p.38.
6. Ossie Enekwe, "Chinua Achebe's Short Stories," p.38.
7. Odun Balogun, *Tradition and Modernity in the African Short Story*, p.97.
8. Odun Balogun, *Tradition and Modernity in the African Short Story*, p.99.
9. Chinua Achebe, *Girls at War and Other Stories*, p.38.
10. For detailed discussions of the uses of similar techniques around the world, see the essays collected in Margaret Reed MacDonald, ed. *Traditional Storytelling Today*, 1999.
11. For an account of similar circumstances of disinheritance caused by Euoropeanization, see Cheikh Hamidou Kane, *Ambiquous Adventures*.
12. Achebe, *Girls at War and Other Stories*, p.38.
13. Ibid. p.43.
14. Ibid. pp.44-45.
15. Ibid. p.46.

16. Ibid. p.47.
17. There has been considerable debate regarding the quality of parody in *A Man of the People*, but I do not think there can be any doubt about its effectiveness in "Uncle Ben's Choice."
18. Achebe, *Girls at War and Other Stories*, p.76.
19. Ibid. p.77
20. Ibid. p.78.
21. Ibid. p.78.
22. Ibid. pp.80-81.
23. Ibid. p.14.
24. Ibid. p.18.
25. Ibid. p.69.
26. Ibid. p.65.
27. Ibid. p.111.
28. Ibid. p.106.
29. Ibid. p.108.
30. Ibid. p.105.

CONCLUSION

1. See Odun Balogun, *Ngugi and Postcolonial Narrative* for details.
2. For a full account, see Eileen Julien's discussion in *African Novels and Orality* of the experimental works of Hampate Ba, Camara Laye, Jean-Marie Adiaffi, and Sonny Labou Tabansi.
3. See Isidore Okpewho's 1983 book *Myth in Africa* for an extensive discussion.
4. See Sandra Richards' discussion in *Ancient Songs Set Ablaze* of J. P. Clark-Bedekeremo's resourceful plays.
5. Mariama Ba, *So Long a Letter*.
6. See Femi Osofisan's plays such as *Birthdays Are Not for Dying* and *The Oriki for a Grasshopper*.
7. See Ousmane Sembene, *Xala*, *The Money Order*, and *Gods Bits of Wood*.
8. See Ngugi wa Thiong'o, *Maitigari*, *Devil on the Cross*, and *Petals of Blood*.

BIBLIOGRAPHY

WORKS BY ACHEBE

Achebe, Chinua. "African Literature as Restoration of Celebration," in *Chinua Achebe: A Celebration*, edited by Anna Rutherford and Kirsten Holst Petersen, 1-10 Portsmouth: Heinemann, 1991.

———. *Things Fall Apart.* London: Heinemann, 1958; New York: Astor-Honor, 1959.

———. *No Longer at Ease.* London: Heinemann, 1960; New York: Obolensky, 1961.

———. *The Sacrificial Egg and Other Short Stories.* Onitsha: Etudo, 1962.

———. *Arrow of God.* Rev. ed., London: Heinemann, 1974.

———. *A Man of the People.* London: Heinemann, 1966.

———. *Girls at War and Other Stories.* London: Heinemann, 1972; Garden City, NY.: Anchor/Doubleday, 1973.

———. *Morning Yet On Creation Day: Essays.* London: Heinemann, 1975.

———. *The Trouble with Nigeria.* Enugu: Fourth Dimension, 1983; London: Heinemann, 1983.

———. *Anthills of the Savannah.* London: Heinemann, 1987; New York: Doubleday, 1988.

———. *Hopes and Impediments: Selected Essays, 1965-87.* London: Heinemann, 1988.

———. *Home and Exile.* New York: Oxford University Press, 2000.

SELECTED INTERVIEWS
Lindfors, Bernth, Ian Munro, Richard Priebe, and Reinhard Sander, eds. "Interview with Chinua Achebe." *Palaver: Interviews with Five African Writers.* African and Afro-American Research Institute, University of Texas at Austin, 1972: 5-12.

Nwachukwu Agbada, "A Conversation with Chinua Achebe." *Commonwealth: Essays and Studies.* 13.1 (1990): 117-124.

CRITICAL WORKS

Adebayo, Tunji. "The Past and the Present in Chinua Achebe's Novels." *Ife African Studies* 1. 1 (1974): 66-84.

Adeeko, Adeleke. "Contests of Text and Context in Chinua Achebe's *Arrow of God." Ariel* 23. 2 (April, 1992): 7-22.

Aizenberg, Edna. "The Third World Novel as Counterhistory: *Things Fall Apart* and Asturias's *Men of Maize.*" In Bernth Lindfors, ed., *Approaches to Teaching Achebe's Things Fall Apart.* 85-90.

Alden, Patricia. "New Women and Old Myths: Chinua Achebe's *Anthills of the Savannah.*" *Matatu* 8 (1991): 67-80.

Ascherson, Neil. "Betrayal: *Anthills of the Savannah*" (review) *New York Review of Books* (3 March, 1988): 3-4.

Boafo, Y. S. Kantanka. "*Arrow of God:* A Case Study of Megalomania." *Asemka* 1.2 (1974): 16-24.

Boehmer, Elleke. "Of Goddesses and Stories: Gender and a New Politics in Achebe's Anthills of the Savannah. In *Chinua Achebe: A Celebration*, edited by Kirsten Holst Petersen and Anna Rutherford. 102-112.

Brown, H.R. "Igbo Words for the non-Igbo: Achehe's Artistry in *Arrow of God." Research in African Literatures* 12.1 (Spring, 1981): 69-85.

Brown, Lloyd W. "Cultural Norms and Modes of Perception in Achehe's Fiction." *Research in African Literatures* 3 (1972): 21-35. Rpt. In *Critical Perspectives on Chinua Achebe*, edited by C. L. Innes and Bernth Lindfors.

Carroll, David, *Chinua Achebe.* Rev. ed. New York: Twayne, 1970. London: Macmillan, 1980, 1990.

Cobham, Rhonda. "Making Men and History: Achebe and the Politics of Revision." In Bernth Lindfors, ed., *Approaches to Teaching Things Fall Apart.* New York: Modern Languages Association, 1991. 91-100.

Colmer, Rosemary. "Quis Custodiet? The Developement of Moral Values in *A man of the People.*" In *Chinua Achebe: A Celebration*, edited by Kirsten Holst Petersen and Anna Rutherford. Portsmouth: Heinemann, 1991: 89-101.

Echeruo, M.J.C. "Chinua Achebe." In *A Celebration of Black and African Writing*, edited by Bruce King and Kolawole Ogungbesan, Zaria and Ibadan: Ahmadu Bello University Press and Oxford University Press, 1975. 150-63.

Egudu, R.N. "Achebe and the Igbo Narrative Tradition." *Research in African Literatures* 12 (Spring, 1981): 43-54.

Eko, Ebele. "Chinua Achebe and His Critics: Reception of His Novels in English and American Reviews." *Studies in Black Literature* 6. 3 (1975): 14-20.

Elder, Arlene. "The Paradoxical Characterization of Okonkwo." In Bernth Lindfors, ed., *Approaches to Teaching Things Fall Apart.* 58-64.

Emenyonu, Ernest. "Ezeulu: The Night Mask Caught Abroad by Day."
   Pan African Journal 4 (1971): 407-19.

———. "Chinua Achebe's *Things Fall Apart*: A Classic Study in Colonial Diplomatic Tactlessness." In Kirsten Holst Petersen and Anna
   Rutherford, eds., *Chinua Achebe: A Celebration.* 83-88.

Enekwe, Ossie. "Chinua Achebe's Short Stories." *Nigerian Literature
   1700 to the Present Volume Two*, edited by Yemi Ogunbiyi. Lagos:
   Guardian Books, 1988. 38-42.

Gikandi, Simon. "Chinua Achebe and the Signs of the Times." In Lindfors,
   ed. *Approaches to Teaching Things Fall Apart.* 25-30.

———. *Reading Chinua Achebe: Language and Ideology in Fiction.*
   London: James Currey, 1991.

Gordimer, Nadine. "A Tyranny of Clowns" (Review of *Anthills of the Savannah*). *New York Times Book Review* (21 February 1988): 1, 26.

Gowdah, H.H. "The Novels of Chinua Achebe." *Literary Half-Yearly* 14. 2
   (1973): 3-9.

Griffiths, Gareth. "Language and Action in the Novels of Chinua
   Achebe."*African Literature Today* 5 (1971): 88-105. Rpt. In C. L .
   Innes and Bernth Lindfors, eds., *Critical Perspectives on Chinua
   Achebe.*

Heywood, Christopher. "Surface and Symbol in *Things Fall Apart.*" *Journal of the Nigerian English Studies Association* (1967): 41-5.

Ikegami, Robin. "Knowledge and Power, The Story and The Storyteller:
   Achebe's *Anthills of the Savannah.*" *Modern Fiction Studies* 37.3
   (1991): 493-507.

Innes, C.L. *Chinua Achebe.* Cambridge: Cambridge University Press, 1990.

———. and Bernth Lindfors, eds., *Critical Perspectives on Chinua
   Achebe.* Washington DC: Three Continents Press, 1978; London:
   Heinemann, 1979.

Irele, Abiola."The Tragic Conflict in Achehe's Novels." *Black Orpheus* 17
   (1965): 24-32. Rpt. in C. L. Innes and Bernth Lindfors, eds., *Critical
   Perspectives on Chinua Achebe.*

Iyasere, Solomon. "Narrative Techniques in *Things Fall Apart.*" *New Letters* 40 (1974): 73-93. Rpt. in C. L. Innes and Bernth Lindfors, eds.,
   Critical Perspectives in Chinua Achebe.

Izevbaye, Dan."The Igbo as Exceptional Subjects: Fictionalizing an Ab-
   normal Historical Situation." In Bernth Lindfors, ed., *Approaches to
   Teaching Achebe's Things Fall Apart.* 45-51.

Jabbi, Buabeki. "Myth in *Arrow of God.*" *African Literarure Today* 11(1980):
   130-148.

Jan Mohamed, Abdul R."Sophisticated primitivism: the Syncretism of
   Oral and Literate Modes in Achehe's *Things Fall Apart.*" *Ariel* 15.4

(1984): 19-39.

Jeyifo, Biodun. "For Chinua Achebe: The Resilience and the Predicament of Obierika." *Kunapipi* 12.2 (1990): 51-70.

Killam, G.D. *The Writings of Chinua Achebe*, Rev. ed. London: Heinemann, 1977.

_____. "Notions of Religion, Alienation and Archetype in *Arrow of God.*" In *Exile and Tradition: Studies in African and Caribbean Literature*, edited by Rowland Smith. New York: Africana Publishing Co. and Halifax, Canada: Dalhousie University Press, 1976. 152-65.

King, Bruce. "The Revised *Arrow of God.*" *African Literature Today* 13 (1983): 69-78.

Kronenfeld, J. Z. "The 'Communalistic' African and the 'Individualistic' Westerner: Some Comments on Misleading Generalizations in Western Criticism of Soyinka and Achebe." *Research in African Literatures* 6 (1975): 199-225.

Kuesgen, Reinhardt. "Conrad and Achebe: Aspects of the Novel." *WLWE* 24 (Summer 1984): 27-33.

Lewis, Mary Ellen B. "Beyond Content in the Analysis of Folklore in Literature: Chinua Achehe's *Arrow of God.*" *Research in African Literatures* 7 (1976): 44-52.

Lindfors, Bernth. "Achebe's African Parable." *Presence Africaine* 66 (1968): 130-66. Rpt. in C. L. Innes and Bernth Lindfors, eds., *Critical Perspectives on Chinua Achebe*.

————."The Palm Oil with Which Achebe's Words Are Eaten." *African Literature Today* 1 (1968), 3-18. Rpt. in C. L. Innes and Bernth Lindfors, eds., *Critical Perspectives on Chinua Achebe*.

————, ed., *Approaches to Teaching Achebe's Things Fall Apart*. New York: Modern Languages Association, 1991.

————, and Ulla Schild, ed., *Neo-African Literature and Culture: Essays in Memory of Janheinz Jahn*. Wiesbaden: B.Heyman Verlag GmbH, 1976.

Mahood, M.M. "Idols of the Den." *The Colonial Encounter*. London: Rex Coilings, 1976. Rpt. in C. L. Innes and Bernth Lindfors, eds. *Critical Perspectives on Chinua Achebe*.

Maughan-Brown, David. "*Anthills of the Savannah* and the Ideology of Leadership."*Matatu* 8 (1991): 3-22.

Melamu, M, J. "The Quest for Power in Achebe's *Arrow of God.*" *English Studies in Africa* 14 (1971): 225-40.

Muonoke, Romanus Okey. *Art, Rebellion and Redemption: A Reading of the Novels of Chinua Achebe*. New York: Peter Lang, 1994.

Narasimhaiah, C., ed. *Awakened Conscience: Studies in Commonwealth Literature*. New Delhi: Sterling, 1978 .

Ngara, Emmanuel. "Achebe as Artist: The Place and Significance of *Ant-hills of the Savannah* ." In Kirsten Holst Petersen and Anna Ruther-ford, eds., *Chinua Achebe: A Celebration.*

Ngugi wa Thiong'o [James]. "Chinua Achebe: *A Man of the People.*" *Homecoming: Essays on Africa and Caribbean Literature, Culture and Politics.* London: Heinemann, 1972; Rpt. in C. L. Innes and Bernth Lindfors, eds., *Critical Perspectives on Chinua Achebe.*

Niven, Alastair. "Another Look at *Arrow of God.*" *Literary Half-Yearly* 16. 2 (1975): 53-68.

———. "Chinua Achebe and the Possibility of Modern Tragedy." In Kirsten Holst Petersen and Anna Rutherford, eds., *Chinua Achebe: A Celebration.* 41-50.

Njoku, Benedict. *The Four Novels of Chinua Achebe: A Critical Study.* New York: Peter Lang, 1984.

Nnadozie, F. Inyama. "Genetic Discontinuty in *No Longer at Ease.*" In Kalu Ogba, ed., *The Gong and the Flute. African Literary Develop-ment and Celebration.* 119-127.

Nnolim, C.E. "Achebe's *Things Fall Apart*: An Igbo National Epic." *Black Academy Review* 2.1/2 (1971):55-60.

———. "A Source for *Arrow of God.*" *Research in African Literatures* 8 (1977):1-26.

———. "Form and Function of the Folk Tradition in Achehe's Novels." *Ariel* 14 (1983): 35-47.

———. "The Sons of Achebe." *Kriteria* 1.1 (1988): 1-14.

Nwachukwu-Agbada, J. O. J. "Chinua Achebe's Literary Proverbs as Re-flections of Igbo Cultural and Philosophical Tenets."*Proverbium* 10 (1993): 215-235.

Nwoga, D. I. 'The Igbo World of Achebe's *Arrow of God.*" *Research in African Literatures* 12 (Spring 1981): 14-42.

Obiechina, Emmanuel."Post-Independence Disillusionment in Three Afri-can Novels." In Ulla Schild and Bernth Lindfors, eds., *Neo-African Literature and Culture: Essays in Memory of Janheinz Jahn.* 119-146.

Ogede, Ode S. Review of Simon Gikandi's *Reading Chinua Achebe. Af-rica* 62. 3 (1992): 457-59.

———. "Achebe and Armah: A Unity of Shaping Visions." *Research in African Literatures* 27.2 (1996): 112-27.

Ogu, J. N. "The Concept of Madness in Chinua Achehe's Writings." *Jour-nal of Commonwealth Literature* 18.1 (1983): 48-54.

Ogungbesan, Kolawole. "Politics and the African Writer: The Example of Chinua Achebe." *Work in Progress* (Zaria) 2 (1973): 75-93 and *African*

Studies Review 17 (1974): 43-54. Rpt. in C. L. Innes and Bernth Lindfors, eds., *Critical Perspectives on Chinua Achebe.*

Oko, Emelia A. "The Historical Novel of Africa: A Sociological Approach to Achebe's *Things Fall Apart* and *Arrow of God.*" *Conch* 6, 1/2 (1974): 15-46.

Okpaku, Joseph. "A Novel for the People." *Journal of the New African Literature* 2 (Fall 1966): 76-80.

Olney, James. "The African Novel in Transition: Chinua Achebe." *South Atlantic Quarterly* 70 (1971): 229-316.

Owusu, Kofi. "The Politics of Interpretation: The Novels of Chinua Achebe." *Modern Fiction Studies* 37.3 (1991): 459-470.

Peters, Jonathan. *A Dance of Masks: Senghor, Achebe, Soyinka.* Washington DC: Three Continents Press, 1975.

Pieterse, Cosmo and Donald Munro, eds., *Protest and Conflict in African Literature.* London: Heinemann; New York: Africana Publishing, 1969

Ravenscroft, Arthur. *Chinua Achebe.* Harlow: Longmans, the National Book, 1969; Rev. ed., 1977.

Riddy, Felicity. "Language as a Theme in *No Longer At Ease.*" *Journal of Commonwealth Literature* 9 (1970): 38-47. Rpt. in C. L. Innes Bernth and Lindfors, eds., *Critical Perspectives on Chinua Achebe.*

Rodney, Walter. *How Europe Underdeveloped Africa.* Washington, DC.: Howard University Press, 1982.

Rogers, Philip. "*No Longer at Ease*: Chinua Achebe's Heart of W h i t e - ness." *Research in African Literatures* 14 (Summer,1983):165-83.

Scheub, Harold. "When a Man Fails Alone." *Presence Africaine* 74 (1970): 61-89.

Serumaga, Robert. "A Mirror of Integration: Chinua Achebe and James Ngugi." In Cosmo Pieterse and Donald Munro, eds., *Protest and Conflict in African Literature.* 70-80.

Stock, A.G. "Yeats and Achebe." *Journal of Commonwealth Literature* 5 (1968): 105-11. Rpt. in C. L. Innes and Bernth Lindfors, eds., *Critical Perspectives on Chinua Achebe.*

ten Kortenar, Neil. "Beyond Authenticity and Creolization: Reading Achebe Writing Culture." *PMLA* 110 (January,1995): 30-42.

Udumukwu, Onyemaechi. "Achebe and the Negation of Independence." *Modern Fiction Studies* 37.3 (1991): 471-91.

Vincent, Theo. "Register in Achebe." *Journal of the Nigerian English Studies Association* 6.1 (1974): 95-106.

Wanjala, Chris L. "Achebe: Teacher and Satirist." in *Standpoints in African Literature: A Critical Anthology.* 161-71.

———, ed., *Standpoints in African Literature: A Critical Anthology.* Nairobi: East African Literature Bureau, 1973.

Weinstock, Donald and Cathy Ramadan. "Symbolic Structure in *Things Fall Apart.*" *Critique* 11, 1 (1969): 33-41. Rpt. in C. L. Innes and Bernth Lindfors, ed. *Critical Perspectives on Chinua Achebe.*

Wilson, Roderick. "Eliot and Achebe: An Analysis of Some Formal and Philosophical Qualities of *No Longer at Ease.*" *Enghsh Studies in Africa* 14 (1971): 215-23. Rpt. in C. L. Innes and Bernth   Lindfors, eds., *Critical Perspectives on Chinua Achebe.*

Winters, M. "An Objective Approach to Achebe's Style." *Research in African Literatures* 12 (Spring 1981): 55-68.

Wren, Robert. *Achehe's World: The Historical and Cultural Context of the Novels of Chinua Achebe.* Washington, DC.: Three Continents Press, 1980.

———. "*Things Fall Apart* in Its Time and Place." In Bernth Lindfors, ed. *Approaches to Teaching Things Fall Apart.* 38-44.

———. "*Mister Johnson* and the Complexity *of Arrow of God.*" In *Awakened Conscience: Studies in Commonwealth Literature*, C. Narasimhaiah, ed. 50-62. Rpt. in C. L. Innes and Bernth Lindfors, eds., *Critical Perspectives on Chinua Achebe.*

Yankson, Kofi. *Chinua Achebe's Novels: A Socio-linguistic Perspective.* Uruowulu-Obosi: Pacific Publishers, 1990.

———. "The Use of Pidgin in *No Longer at Ease* and A *Man of the People.*" *Asemka* 1. 2 (1974): 68-79.

GENERAL WORKS

Abrahams, Peter. *Tell Freedom.* London: Faber, 1954.

Achebe, Chinua. "An Image of Africa: Racism in Conrad's *Heart of Darkness.*" *Massachusetts Review* 18 (1977): 782-94. Rept. in *Chant of Saints: A Gathering of Afro-American Literature, Art, andScholarship*, edited by Michael S. Harper and Robert Stepto. Urbana: University of Illinois Press, 1979. 313-25.

Aidoo, Ama Ata. *The Dilemma of a Ghost.* Harlow, England: Longman,1965.

———. *No Sweetness Here.* Harlow, England: Longman, 1970.

Afigbo, A. E . *Warrant Chiefs: Indirect Rule in Southern Nigeria.* London: Longman, 1972.

Amuta, Chidi. "Literature of the Nigerian Civil War." In Yemi Ogunbiyi, ed., *Perspectives on Nigerian Literature 1700 to the Present: Volume 1.* Lagos: Guardian Books, 1988. 85-92.

Anene, J. C. *Southern Nigeria in Transition 1885-1906.* Cambridge: Cambridge University Press, 1966.

Anozie, Sunday. *Christopher Okigbo: Creative Rhetoric.* London: Evans Brothers, 1972.

———. *Structural Models and African Poetics.* London: Routledge &

Kegan Paul, 1981.

Armah, Ayi Kwei. *The Beautyful Ones Are Not Yet Born*. London: Heinemann, 1969.

———. *The Healers*. London: Heinemann, 1978.

———. *Two Thousand Seasons*. London: Heinemann, 1979.

———. *The Healers*. London: Heinemann, 1979.

Asante, S. K. B. "Obituary Ras Makonen." *West Africa* (24 September, 1984): 1944.

Aschcroft, Bill, Gareth Griffiths and Helen Tiffin. *The Empire Writes Back: Theory and Practice in Post-colonial Writing*. New Accents. London/New York: Routledge, 1989.

Asien, Omo. S. "Literature and Society in Lagos in the Early 20th Century." *Nigeria Magazine* 117-18 (1975): 22-32.

Atkins, Keletso E. *The Moon Is Dead! Give Us Our Money! The Cultural Origins of an African Work Ethic, Natal South Africa, 1843-1900*. Portsmouth, NH.: Heinemann, 1993.

Auerbarch, Eric. *Mimesis: The Representation of Reality in Western Literature*. Translated by Willard Trask. Princeton: Princeton University Press, 1953.

Awoonor, Kofi. *The Breast of the Earth*. New York: NOK, 1975.

———. *This Earth, My Brother...* London: Heinemann,1972.

Balogun, Odun F. *Tradition and Modernity in the African Short Story: An Introduction to a Literature in Search of Critics*. New York: Greenwood Press, 1991.

———. *Ngugi and the African Postcolonial Narrative: The Novel as Oral Narrative in Multigenre Performance*. Quebec, Canada: World Heritage Press, 1997.

Barber, Karin. *I Could Speak Until Tomorrow: Oriki, Women and the Past in a Yoruba Town*. Washington, DC.: Smithsonian Institution Press, 1991.

Barthes, Roland. *The Rustle of Language*. Translated by Richard Howard. Berekely and Los Angeles: University of California Press, 1989.

Berzon, Judith, R. *Neither White nor Black: The Mulatto Character in American Fiction*. New York: New York University Press, 1978.

Beti, Mongo. *Mission to Kala*. Translated by Peter Green. London: Heinemann, 1964.

———. *The Poor Christ of Bomba*. 1956. Translated by Gerald Moore. London: Heinemann, 1971.

Bjornson, Richard. *The African Quest for Freedom and Identity: Cameroonian Writing and the National Experience*. Bloomington: Indiana University Press, 1991.

Boahen, Adu. A. *African Perpectives on Colonialism*. Baltimore: Johns Hopkins University Press, 1987.

Booth, James. *Writers and Politics in Nigeria*. London: Hodder & Stoughton, 1981.

Bowersock, G. W. *Fiction as History*. Berkeley: University of California Press, 1994.

Brydon, Diana. "The Myths that Write Us: Decolonizing the Mind." *Commonwealth: Essays and Studies* 10 (1987): 1-14.

Busia, Abena. "Imagined Communities and Fixed Boundaries." *African Literature Association Bulletin* 19.3 (1993): 7-13.

Byerman, Keith. E. *Fingering the Jagged Grain: Tradition and Form in Recent Black Fiction*. Athens: University of Georgia Press, 1986.

Cabral, Amilcar. *Revolution in Guinea*. New York: Monthly Review, 1972.
———. *Return to the Source*. New York: Monthly Review, 1973.

Carmichael, Stokely and Charles V. Hamilton. *Black Power: The Politics of Liberation in America*. Harmondsworth: Pelican, 1969.

Chambers, Ross. *Room for Manuever: Reading (the) Oppositional (in) Narrative*. Chicago: The University of Chicago Press, 1991.

Clark, John Pepper. *America, Their America*. London: Andre Deutsch, 1964.

Comaroff, Jean and John. *Of Revelation and Revolution: Christianity, Colonialism, and Consciousness in South Africa*. Chicago: University of Chicago Press, 1991.

———. *Of Revelation and Revolution: Christianity, Colonialism, and Consciousness in South Africa Volume II*. Chicago: University of Chicago Press, 1997.

Comaroff, Jean. *Body of Power, Spirit of Resistance: The Culture and History of a South African People*. Chicago: University of Chicago Press, 1985.

Conteh-Morgan, John. *Theatre and Drama in Francophone Africa*. Cambridge: Cambridge University Press, 1994.

Conrad, Joseph. *Heart of Darkness*. New York: Harper & Brothers, 1910.

Cook, David. *African Literature: A Critical View*. London: Longman, 1977.

Corkey, Daniel. *Synge and Anglo-Irish Literature*. Cork, Ireland: Cork University Press, 1931.

D' Almeida, Irene Assiba. *Francophone African Women Writers: Destroying the Emptiness of Silence*. Gainesville: University Press of Florida, 1994.

de Lauretis, Teresa. *Alice Doesn't: Feminism, Semiotics, Cinema*. Bloomington: Indiana University Press, 1984.

Dathorne, O.R. *African Literature in the Twentieth Century*. London:

Heinemann, 1976.

Davidson, Basil. A. "African Resistance and Rebellion against the Imposition of Colonial Rule." In T. O. Ranger, ed. *Emerging Themes of African History*. Nairobi: East African Publishing House, 1968. 177-188.

Diop, Cheikh Anta. *The African Origin of Civilisation: Myth or Reality*. Translated by Mercer Cook. Westport: Laurence Hill, 1974.

Duerden, Dennis. *African Art and Literature: The Invisible Present*. London: Heinemann, 1975.

Dyer, Richard. *White*. London: Routledge, 1997.

Eagleton, Terry. *Literary Theory: An Introduction*. Minneapolis: University of Minnesota Press, 1983.

Edmondson, Belinda. *Making Men: Gender, Literary Authority, and Women's Writing in Caribbean Narrative*. Durham, NC.: Duke University Press, 1999.

Ekechi, F. K. *Missionary Enterprise and Rivalry in Igboland 1857-1914*. London: Frank Cass, 1972.

Eliot, T. S . "Tradition and the Individual Talent." *Selected Prose of Elliot*, edited by Frank Kermode. London: Faber, 1975.

Emecheta, Buchi. *The Rape of Shavi*. New York: George Braziller, 1985.

Fanon, Frantz. *A Dying Colonialism*. Translated by Haakon Chevalier. New York: Grove Press, 1967.

———. *Black Skin, White Masks*. Translated by Charles Lam Markmann. New York: Grove Press, 1967.

———. *The Wretched of the Earth*. Translated by Constance Farrington. Harmondsworth, England: Penguin, 1967.

Finnegan, Ruth. *Oral Literature in Africa*. London: Oxford University Press, 1970.

Furst, Lilian R. *All Is True: The Claims and Strategies of Realist Fiction*. Durham, NC.: Duke University Press, 1995.

Gates, Henry Louis, Jr. *Figures in Black: Words, Signs, and the Racial Self*. New York: Oxford University Press, 1987.

———. "On the Rhetoric of Racism in the Profession." *African Literature Association Bulletin* 15.1(1989):11-21.

———. *The Signifying Monkey: A Theory of African-American Literary Criticism*. New York and Oxford: Oxford University Press, 1988.

Gakwandi, Shatto Arthur. *The Novel and Contemporary Experience in Africa*. London: Heinemann, 1977.

Gikandi, Simon. *Reading the African Novel*. London: James Currey, 1987.

Goodwin, Ken. *Understanding African Poetry: A Study of Ten Poets*. London: Heinemann, 1982.

Goody, Jack. *The Domestication of the Savage Mind*. Cambridge: Cambridge University Press, 1977.

Griffiths, Gareth. *A Double Exile: African and West Indian Writing Between Two Cultures.* London: Marion Boyars, 1978.

Hardy, Thomas. *The Mayor of Casterbridge.* London: Macmillan, 1974.

Hargreaves, John D. *West Africa Partitioned: Volume II, The Elephant and the Grass.* Madison: University of Wisconsin Press, 1985.

Harrow, Kenneth. *Thresholds of Change in African Literature: The Emergence of a Tradition.* Portsmouth: Heinemann, 1994.

Harlow, Barbara. *Resistance Literature.* New York and London: Methuen, 1987.

Heron, G. A. *The Poetry of Okot p'Bitek.* London: Heinemann, 1976.

Heyne, Eric. "Towards a Theory of Literary Non-Fiction." *Modern Fiction Studies* 33.3 (1987): 479-90.

Holloway, Karla. F. C. *Moorings and Metaphors: Figures of Culture and Gender in Black Women's Literature.* New Brunswick, NJ.: Rutgers University Press, 1992.

Ikime, Obaro. *The Fall of Nigeria.* London: Heinemann Educational Books, 1977.

Irele, Abiola. *The African Experience in Literature and Ideology.* London: Heinemann, 1981.

Isichei, Elizabeth. *A History of the Igbo People.* London: Macmillan, 1976.
———. *Igbo World.* London: Macmillan, 1977.
———. *The Ibo People and the Europeans.* London: Faber and Faber, 1973.

Iyayi, Festus. *Heroes.* London: Longman, 1986.
———. *Violence.* London: Longman, 1979.

Izevbaye, D . S. "The State of Criticism in African Literature." *African Literature Today* 7 (1975): 1-19.

Jameson, Fredric. *The Political Unconscious: Narrative as a Socially Symbolic Act.* Ithaca, New York: Cornell University Press, 1981.

Jones, Eldred, Eustace Palmer and Marjorie Jones, eds., *Orature in African Literature Today:ALT 18.* London: James Currey, 1992.

Julien, Eileen. *African Novels and the Question of Orality.* Bloomington and Indianapolis: Indiana University Press, 1992.

Kane, Hamidou. *Ambiquous Adventures.* London: Heinemann, 1961.

Killam, G. D., ed., *Critical Perspectives on Ngugi wa Thiongo.* Washington, DC.: Three Continents Press, 1984.

King, Bruce. Review of Robert Wren, *Those Magical Years: The Making of Nigerian Literature at Ibadan. Ariel* 24. 4 (1993): 118-122.

Kourouma, Ahmadu. *Les Soliels des independences.* Paris: Editions du Seuil, (1968), 1970.

Krieger, Murray. *The Institution of Theory.* Baltimore and London: Johns

Hopkins University Press, 1994.

Kunene, Daniel. *The Heroic Poetry of the Basotho*. Oxford: Clarendon Press, 1971.

Landau, Paul Stuart. *The Realm of the Word: Language, Gender, and Christianity in a Southern African Kingdom*. Portsmouth, NH.: Heinemann, 1995.

Larson, Charles. *The Emergence of African Fiction*. Bloomington and London: Indiana University Press, 1971. Rev. ed., London: Macmillan, 1978.

————, ed. *Modern African Stories*. London: Collins/Fontana, 1971.

Lawrence, D. H. *Lady Charterly's Lover*. 1928. New York: Grove Press, 1957.

Lawson, William. *The Western Scar: The Theme of the Been-to in West African Fiction*. Athens: Ohio University Press, 1982.

Laye, Camara. *The African Child*. 1955. Translated by James Kirkup, London: Collins/Fontana, 1965.

————. *The Radiance of the King*. 1954. Translated by James Kirkup. New York: Collier Books, 1971.

Lentricchia, Frank and Thomas McLaughlin, eds., *Critical Terms for Literary Study*. Chicago: University of Chicago Press, 1990.

Lewis, Benard. *Race and Slavery in the Middle East: An Historical Enquiry*. New York: Oxford University Press, 1990.

Lindfors, Bernth. *Folklore in Nigerian Literature*. New York: Africana, 1973.

————, and Oyekan Owomoyela, eds. *Yoruba Proverbs*. Athens: Ohio University Center for International Studies, Africa Program, 1973.

Lipking, Lawrence. *The Life of the Poet: Beginning and Ending Poetic Careers*. Chicago: The University of Chicago Press, 1981.

MacDonald, Margaret Reed, ed., *Traditional Storytelling Today: An International Sourcebook*. Chicago: Fitzroy Dearborn, 1999.

Madeline, Cottenet-Hage and Kevin Meehan. "Our Ancestors the Gauls. . . 'Schools and Schooling'." *Callaloo* 15.1(1992): 75-89.

Mafeje, Archie. "The Role of the Bard in a Contemporary African Community." *Journal of African Languages* 6 (1967): 193-223.

Maja-Pearce, Adewale. *A Mask Dancing: Nigerian Novelists of the Eighties*. London: Hans Zell, 1992.

Mamdani, Mahmood. *Citizen and Subject: Contemporary Africa and the Legacy of Late Colonialism*. Princeton, NJ.: Princeton University Press, 1996.

Mazrui, Ali. *The Trial of Christopher Okigbo*. London: Heinemann, 1971.

McEwan, Nell. *Africa and the Novel*. London: Macmillan, 1983.

Melville, Herman. *Moby-Dick*. 1851. Reprint. New York: New American

Index